WITHDRAWAL

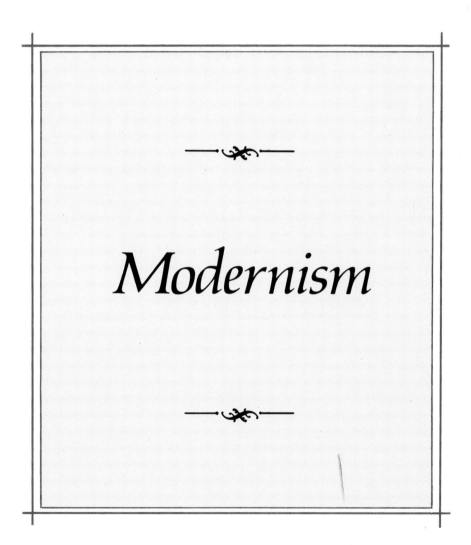

Modernism

GREAT ARTISTS OF THE WESTERN WORLD

Modernism

Henri Matisse

—❧—

Pablo Picasso

—❧—

Umberto Boccioni

—❧—

Amedeo Modigliani

MARSHALL CAVENDISH · LONDON · NEW YORK · SYDNEY

Staff Credits

Editors	Clive Gregory LL B Sue Lyon BA (Honours)	**Picture Researchers**	Vanessa Fletcher BA (Honours) Flavia Howard BA (Honours) Jessica Johnson BA
Art Editors	Kate Sprawson BA (Honours) Keith Vollans LSIAD	**Production Controllers**	Steve Roberts Alan Stewart BSc
Deputy Editor	John Kirkwood B Sc (Honours)	**Secretary**	Lynn Smail
Sub-editors	Caroline Bugler BA (Honours), MA Sue Churchill BA (Honours) Alison Cole BA, M Phil Jenny Mohammadi Nigel Rodgers BA (Honours), MA Penny Smith Will Steeds BA (Honours), MA	**Publisher**	Terry Waters Grad IOP
		Editorial Director	Maggi McCormick
		Production Executive	Robert Paulley B Sc
Designers	Stuart John Julie Stanniland	**Consultant and Authenticator**	Sharon Fermor BA (Honours) Lecturer in the Extra-Mural Department of London University and Lecturer in Art History at Sussex University

Reference Edition 2001

Marshall Cavendish Corporation
99 White Plains Road
Tarrytown, NY 10591-9001

Printed in Malaysia

Library of Congress Cataloging-in-Publication Data

Great Artists of the Western World.

Includes index.
1. Artists—Biography. I. Marshall Cavendish Corporation
N40.G77 1987   709'.2'2 [B]   86—23863

ISBN 0-86307-743-9 (set)
0-86307-751-X (vol. 8)

Preface

Looking at pictures can be one of the greatest pleasures that life has to offer. Note, however, those two words 'can be'; all too many of us remember all too clearly those grim afternoons of childhood when we were dragged, bored to tears and complaining bitterly, through room after room of Italian primitives by well-meaning relations or tight-lipped teachers. It was enough to put one off pictures for life – which, for some of us, was exactly what it did.

For if gallery-going is to be the fun it should be, certain conditions must be fulfilled. First, the pictures we are to see must be good pictures. Not necessarily great pictures – even a few of these can be daunting, while too many at a time may prove dangerously indigestible. But they must be well-painted, by good artists who know precisely both the effect they want to achieve and how best to achieve it. Second, we must limit ourselves as to quantity. Three rooms – four at the most – of the average gallery are more than enough for one day, and for best results we should always leave while we are still fresh, well before satiety sets in. Now I am well aware that this is a counsel of perfection: sometimes, in the case of a visiting exhibition or, perhaps, when we are in a foreign city with only a day to spare, we shall have no choice but to grit our teeth and stagger on to the end. But we shall not enjoy ourselves quite so much, nor will the pictures remain so long or so clearly in our memory.

The third condition is all-important: we must know something about the painters whose work we are looking at. And this is where this magnificent series of volumes – one of which you now hold in your hands – can make all the difference. No painting is an island: it must, if it is to be worth a moment's attention, express something of the personality of its painter. And that painter, however individual a genius, cannot but reflect the country, style and period, together with the views and attitudes of the people among whom he or she was born and bred. Even a superficial understanding of these things will illuminate a painting for us far better than any number of spotlights, and if in addition we have learnt something about the artist as a person – life and loves, character and beliefs, friends and patrons, and the places to which he or she travelled – the interest and pleasure that the work will give us will be multiplied a hundredfold.

Great Artists of the Western World will provide you with just such an insight into the life and work of some of the outstanding painters of Europe and America. The text is informative without ever becoming dry or academic, not limiting itself to the usual potted biographies but forever branching out into the contemporary world outside and beyond workshop or studio. The illustrations, in colour throughout, have been dispensed in almost reckless profusion. For those who, like me, revel in playing the Attribution Game – the object of which is to guess the painter of each picture before allowing one's eye to drop to the label – the little sections on 'Trademarks' are a particularly happy feature; but every aficionado will have particular preferences, and I doubt whether there is an art historian alive, however distinguished, who would not find some fascinating nugget of previously unknown information among the pages that follow.

This series, however, is not intended for art historians. It is designed for ordinary people like you and me – and for our older children – who are fully aware that the art galleries of the world constitute a virtually bottomless mine of potential enjoyment, and who are determined to extract as much benefit and advantage from it as they possibly can. All the volumes in this collection will enable us to do just that, expanding our knowledge not only of art itself but also of history, religion, mythology, philosophy, fashion, interior decoration, social customs and a thousand other subjects as well. So let us not simply leave them around, flipping idly through a few of their pages once in a while. Let us read them as they deserve to be read – and welcome a new dimension in our lives.

John Julius Norwich is a writer and broadcaster who has written histories of Venice and of Norman Sicily as well as several works on history, art and architecture. He has also made over twenty documentary films for television, including the recent **Treasure Houses of Britain** series which was widely acclaimed after repeated showings in the United States.

Lord Norwich is Chairman of the Venice in Peril Fund, and member of the Executive Committee of the British National Trust, an independently funded body established for the protection of places of historic interest and natural beauty.

John Julius Norwich

Contents

Introduction

Brera, Milan

Coll Jucker, Milan/Scala

The sensation of speed
*(right) Boccioni was fascinated
by the idea of speed, which he
described as 'the new absolute'.
In this painting* Elasticity
*(1912), the forms of horse and
rider are distorted and merged
with the background to suggest
their velocity.*

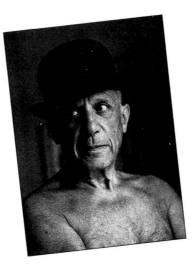

*The development of photography had a tremendous
impact on modern art. On the one hand, it undercut
one of the most fundamental artistic aims – that of
reproducing nature with fidelity. At the same time,
the new images which photography generated acted
as a spur to many painters, aiding them in their
pursuit of new ways to represent reality. This quest
reached a climax in the first decades of the 20th
century. The years leading up to the outbreak of
World War I were among the most exciting in
the history of art, with different groups of painters
– Fauvists, Cubists, Vorticists, Futurists,
Expressionists, and other, less-important groups –
competing to create a new age in art.*

The forum for all this activity was Paris. The French capital, which had gradually established itself as the breeding ground for the avant-garde, became a magnet for aspiring artists from Europe and America. A trip there, at the turn of the century, was as essential as a stay in Rome had been for painters of the 18th century and it is significant that, while only one of the artists in this volume was a native Frenchman, all four regarded acceptance in Paris as the focus of their ambitions.

This community of international talent is collectively known as 'the School of Paris', a deliberately vague term that does not relate to any single style, but is loosely used to cover the Modernist movements that evolved in the first half of the century.

The Fauvist Movement
Paradoxically, though, the earliest of these movements to emerge came from the south rather than the north of France. The immediate stimulus for the Fauvist painters was provided by the warmth of the Mediterranean sun, which Matisse and Derain experienced during their working holiday at Collioure in the summer of 1905. The rich hues that they witnessed and which they sought to recapture are often cited as the inspiration for the 'wild' colouring that gave the group its name.

In fact, there were other precedents for the heightened and non-naturalistic use of colour that characterized the Fauvist style. Gauguin and Van Gogh – who had worked together in the south of France, at Arles – both employed flat areas of pure colour for expressive or symbolic purposes. In addition, Matisse may also have been affected by the cult of Nietzsche, whose writings were available in French by 1898. This charismatic German philosopher acclaimed the joyous, Dionysiac qualities of the south as an antidote to the northern gloom that had dominated the mood of the fin de siècle. The Fauves' sensual approach to art seemed the perfect response to his call for liberation.

The Fauvist movement, spearheaded by Matisse, Vlaminck and Derain, burst upon the Parisian scene in 1905, at the 'Salon d'Automne'. This important exhibiting body had been founded in 1903 as one of the venues where modern art could be displayed. Like the official Salon, it had a jury but, since its members were often associated with avant-garde circles (in 1905, the Vice-President was, like Matisse, an ex-student of Moreau), the selection process was remarkably liberal.

However, while the 1905 showing of the Salon d'Automne brought notoriety to the Fauves, the 1907 exhibition virtually sounded the death-knell of the movement. Then, the memorial show devoted to Cézanne (d.1906) proved a revelation to the art world and shifted the direction of Modernisation away from the Fauves and towards a new style.

Although an extremely short-lived movement, the implications of Fauvism were taken up elsewhere. The German Expressionists, in particular, continued to explore the possibilities of using discordant colour combinations as a means of conveying heightened emotions. Matisse's work had some affinity with this – his wife's portrait, for example (p.23), could easily be mistaken for an Expressionist picture – but his own colour experiments tended to be more decorative. In this, he was strongly influenced by the exhibition of Islamic art in Munich (1910) and by his travels in North Africa.

New Ways of Seeing
Matisse had also been impressed by the Cézanne retrospective in 1907, but the latter's emphasis on structure and form carried far greater significance for the development of Cubism. In his landscapes, Cézanne had stressed the geometric patterns residing in nature, urging his fellow artists to view it in terms of the cone, the cylinder and the sphere.

Picasso seized on this idea, but immediately extended it to include the human figure. Signs of Cézanne's influence could already be discerned in his Demoiselles d'Avignon (pp. 56-7), where the angular distortions of the women's bodies combined with Picasso's growing interest in African

The artists
(far left and right) A photograph of Boccioni, taken in about 1912; a photograph of Picasso from 1963; Modigliani photographed a few months before his death; a self-portrait drawing of Matisse, aged 70.

sculpture to create a revolutionary version of a standard Post-Impressionist theme.

The common factor shared by Cézanne and the African carvings was their reliance on linear simplifications for their effect and it was this approach which Picasso pushed to its logical, if extreme, conclusion. Together with Braque, he evolved a style wherein natural objects were dismantled and then re-assembled in a manner which displayed all their essential structural lines.

Cubism was an unusual movement, inasmuch as it produced no manifesto and its creators worked largely in private. The public face of the style was provided by groups like the Section d'Or, who exhibited far more readily. In time, the disciples of Cubism – such as the Delaunays and Duchamp – led the movement away towards abstraction, although this was a development that Picasso had never intended.

Of course, Picasso's achievements were not confined to a single style. It was a measure of his genius that he left the stamp of his personality on a number of separate art movements, and also that he was able to work concurrently in quite different modes. (His return to a Neo-classical style, for example, coincided with the most sophisticated products of his Cubist phase.)

Picasso's readiness to experiment was his greatest asset. Only three years separated the Women Running on the Beach (pp.60-61) from The Three Dancers (pp.50-51) but, despite the similarity of the themes, his sheer inventiveness had radically altered both the form and the mood of the composition.

A Distinctive Vision
By contrast, Modigliani's artistic ambitions appeared to be contained within a very narrow ambit. In 1907, his interests were identical to those of Picasso – Cézanne and primitive sculpture – but rather than progress from this, he chose to refine these elements into a single, distinctive vision.

Modigliani's career illustrates how very different artistic currents could thrive, side by side, in Paris. While Picasso and the Cubists reigned supreme at the Bateau-Lavoir studios in Montmartre, he gravitated towards La Ruche, south of Montparnesse, where foreign and Jewish artists predominated. Modigliani's closest friends came from this immigrant population and prominent among them were the Russian, Soutine – whose eccentric lifestyle rivalled his own – and the Rumanian sculptor, Brancusi, whose work was to have such a profound effect on the Italian.

In common with other artists in this volume, Modigliani also produced sculpture and, as with Boccioni, it is arguable that his ideas found their fullest expression in this medium. In the remarkable series of Heads (p.111) that he executed between 1910 and 1914, he followed the example of Brancusi and Oceanic sculpture by paring away all extraneous details from the faces to produce a final image of primordial beauty. When he returned to painting in wartime, Modigliani translated this image back onto canvas, imbuing each of his subsequent sitters with the same purity.

Futurism
Modigliani's style had its roots in the past – not only in Oceanic art, but also in the linear tradition of Botticelli and the Florentines – and yet many of the pre-war developments were more iconoclastic. In his native Italy, for instance, the Futurist movement urged the destruction of museums.

In their place, Boccioni and his fellow-Futurists intended to glorify the modern world, symbolized for them by the speed and power of new technology. Like the Cubists, they also aimed to capture, in a single image, a natural effect that could not adequately be conveyed on photographic film – in this case, the sensation of force and movement. Aptly, though, they did make use of photography, as Balla's divisionist rendering of a Muybridge motion study demonstrates (p.100).

The stylistic basis of Futurism was Cubism and, once again, the influence of Paris was decisive. Encouraged by Severini, Boccioni travelled there at the end of 1911, expecting to cause a stir among avant-garde circles. Instead, the reverse happened and he was overwhelmed by the achievements of Picasso, Braque and Delaunay. From them, he derived the interlocking spiral forms that were the basis of his Dynamism series.

Boccioni's career was cut short by his untimely death in 1916; just one of the many watersheds that occurred during World War 1. Movements such as Vorticism and Futurism were effectively curtailed, as were individual groups like Der Blaue Reiter and the Section d'Or. In addition, Picasso discontinued his collaboration with Braque, and Modigliani was forced to abandon sculpture. The first wave of Modernism had come to an end.

Matisse: self-portrait at 70/Philadelphia Museum of Arts

HENRI MATISSE

1869-1954

Henri Matisse was one of the most innovative artists of this century, equalled only by Picasso. His dazzling experiments with colour marked a turning point in the history of art, and formed the basis for most subsequent artistic developments. Matisse took to painting relatively late in life, while recovering from a brief illness. He immediately found in it both an ideal means of expression and a refuge from everyday existence.

After a short period as leader of the Fauvist movement, Matisse forged his own unique style, combining the simplicity of Cézanne with a brilliantly expressive use of colour. His radiant compositions came increasingly to reflect his own aspirations for a life free from trouble and nervous excitement. In reality, his life was largely uneventful, particularly his last years, spent peacefully in the South of France.

A 'Normal Man' of Genius

Presenting an outward image of a sober professor or businessman, Matisse's appearance belied his conflicts and anxieties which could only be resolved through his art.

revelation to him. He recalled later, 'When I started to paint, I felt transported into a kind of paradise . . . In everyday life, I was usually bored and vexed by the things that people were always telling me I must do. Starting to paint, I felt gloriously free, quiet and alone.'

With his father's permission, Matisse gave up law and set off for Paris again – this time, to study with the fashionable and most successful academic painter of his day, Adolphe Bouguereau. But Matisse was soon to become disillusioned with Bouguereau's facile and repetitive productions. In 1892, he became an unofficial student at the Ecole des Beaux-Arts under the aegis of Gustave Moreau. Moreau was a liberal and open-minded teacher, who encouraged his students to follow their own paths and to paint right from the start of the course to develop their gifts as colourists. He not only urged Matisse to copy Old Masters in the Louvre, but also to go out into the streets and draw, taking his subject-matter from everyday life. Matisse made close friends in Moreau's studio, among them, Albert Marquet, who joined Matisse in 'creating' Fauvism some five years later.

Henri Emile Benoît Matisse was born on 31 December 1869 in the northern French town of Le Cateau, at his maternal grandmother's. Both his parents came from Le Cateau, but had met in Paris where his mother, Anna, had worked as a milliner and Emile, his father, had been a draper's assistant. Shortly after the birth, the family moved to the nearby village of Bohain-en-Vermandois, where Emile set up shop as a druggist and grain merchant. This commercial heritage was to prove useful as, throughout his life, Matisse displayed a keen business acumen.

DISCOVERING ART

At first, Matisse gave little indication of his future brilliance and individuality as an artist. At the age of ten, he attended the *lycée* in the neighbouring town of St Quentin, studying Latin and Greek, and in 1887, was sent to Paris to study law. But it was not until he was nearly 19, that he began to take a serious interest in art. Working as a lawyer's clerk in St Quentin, he attended early morning drawing classes at the Ecole Quentin de la Tour, working assiduously from plaster casts between 6.30 and 7.30 am each day. But it was when he was convalescing from appendicitis the following year that he took up painting, and it came as a

Class of '97
(above) Matisse may well be the student seated third from left (front row) in this group portrait of Gustave Moreau's class. He was much happier under the more imaginative teaching of Moreau than he had been with Bouguereau's insistent academicism.

A taste of the South
(right) Matisse visited Corsica on an extended honeymoon in 1898 where he painted many landscape studies. For a painter, who had grown up in northern France and had been no further south than Brittany, this first experience of the Mediterranean was a revelation: 'I felt a passion for colour developing within me.'

Explorer

Key Dates

Life for Matisse in Paris of the *belle époque* was a struggle. By 1894, he already had a daughter, Marguerite, to support (like much of Matisse's personal life, her origins can only be the subject of conjecture). But gradually, Matisse's relatively unadventurous early works, consisting largely of still-lifes and interiors in subdued colours, began to win him success within the Parisian artistic establishment. Four were exhibited at the 1896 Salon of the Société Nationale des Beaux-Arts and at the end of the exhibition, Matisse was elected an Associate Member of the Société. He looked set on the road to a successful, if unexciting, professional artistic career.

However, Matisse was never one to bow to the dictates of fashion, or the demands of the academic establishment. During the following year, he presented to the Salon an ambitious still-life *The Dining Table* (or *La Desserte*) in an Impressionistic style. Although Impressionism was over twenty

Réunion des Musées Nationaux

Musée d'Orsay, Paris

Early influences
(above) The subject of Henri-Edmond Cross's L'Air du Soir *partly inspired the younger Matisse's* Luxe, Calme et Volupté *(p.18). Matisse met Cross when staying at St Tropez with Signac in 1904. The three artists had much in common, but in spite of the title of Matisse's painting, Cross found him 'madly anxious'.*

On the threshold of fame
(right) Matisse was on the brink of success – and notoriety – when this photo was taken around 1905.

Alvin Langdon Coburn/John Hillelson Agency

'The Wild Beasts'

Fauvism burst on to the Paris scene at the 1905 Salon d'Automne, when Matisse and his friends exhibited a group of explosive and brilliantly-coloured canvases which profoundly shocked the art-going public: the painters were labelled, *'fauves'*, or wild beasts. Fauvism was most concerned with the liberation of colour from its traditional, descriptive role. Inspired by Van Gogh, the Fauves used colour as a purely expressive medium for its emotional effect. Fauvism was short-lived, but its experiments with colour formed the basis for many subsequent developments in 20th-century art.

The birthplace of Fauvism
(right) Much of Matisse's Fauvist technique – inspired by the brilliance of Mediterranean light and colour – was arrived at on his first visit to Collioure.

A Fauve friend
(below) Matisse was joined by André Derain at Collioure. Derain's Pool of London, *in brilliant Fauvist colours, is more a rendering of his sensations than of traditional English light.*

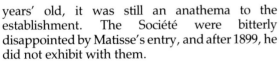

Tate Gallery, London

years' old, it was still an anathema to the establishment. The Société were bitterly disappointed by Matisse's entry, and after 1899, he did not exhibit with them.

The next ten years were years of poverty and hardship for Matisse, lightened only by his marriage in January 1898 to Amélie Parayre, whom he had met a few months before at a wedding. She was to prove a devoted wife and mother – Jean was born in 1899, Pierre, in 1900 – and like Matisse's mother, set herself up as a milliner to support her husband's talent; she also modelled for him for several years. Her love of Oriental patterned fabrics is depicted in her husband's portraits of her in a Japanese kimono. For their honeymoon, they went to London, where Matisse studied the Turners, as advised by Pisarro. On their return to France, they made an extended trip to Corsica – Matisse's first experience of the Mediterranean light and colour, which were to play such an important part in his art.

On their return to Paris, the Matisses set up

home in an apartment on the Quai St Michel, near Matisse's friend, Marquet. Here, Matisse devoted himself to painting and sculpture, and, to alleviate financial difficulties, took a job with a theatrical scene-painter, meticulously painting miles of laurel leaves to decorate the hall then under construction for the 1900 Exposition Universelle.

The first major turning point in Matisse's life came when he and his family spent a summer holiday at St Tropez, near the villas of Paul Signac and Henri-Edmond Cross, two major Neo-Impressionist painters. Under their influence, Matisse began to paint in bright, vivid colours applied in a divisionist technique, which was to culminate in *Luxe, Calme et Volupté* (p.18). The following year, during a summer holiday at Collioure, Matisse produced his first works in the

The last of the Orientalists
(right) In 1911 and 1912, Matisse went to Morocco in search of the exotic. Inspired by the heady colours, he later produced a series of paintings on Oriental themes.

Fauvist style. On his return to Paris, he exhibited several of these paintings, including *The Open Window* (p.22), and a portrait of Madame Matisse in a hat, at the notorious 1905 Salon d'Automne, along with works by Marquet, Vlaminck and Derain. The paintings caused a furore. They were described as 'pictorial aberrations' and 'unspeakable fantasies', and the painters themselves were labelled, *'fauves'* or 'wild beasts', because of the 'savage' colour.

The next major landmark in Matisse's life, was his introduction to the Stein family. Leo, Michael and their more famous authoress sister, Gertrude, were among the most adventurous collectors of the day – and during the next few years they bought many of Matisse's most controversial works. The Steins also introduced him to a circle of enlightened critics, dealers and connoisseurs. Matisse's fortunes improved dramatically – he had acquired discerning patrons at last. He also acquired a regular contract with a prestigious Parisian dealer and moved into a large house with grounds – 'our little Luxembourg' – in the suburbs of Issy-les-Moulineaux. He could travel frequently and made trips to North Africa and Germany where he saw the grand Islamic Exhibition in 1910.

Matisse also attracted the patronage of a rich, cultivated Russian merchant, Sergei Shchukin. Looking more like a Tartar nomad of the Steppes, Shchukin was the ideal patron: not only incredibly wealthy, but unprejudiced and with vision. In 1909, he commissioned two large mural

decorations for his baroque palace of a home in Moscow, including *Dance* (p.21).

Thus, the first decade of the new century was spent in the flush of prosperity, with travels further afield to Russia, Morocco and Spain. However, in 1914 the war temporarily interrupted Matisse's travels. Too old to enlist, it shattered his peace of mind, for he was continually anxious about the fate of his friends. He painted little during the next two years and concentrated instead on etching and devoted himself to the study of the violin. He would joke in later life that it was insurance – if his eye sight failed him, he could always busk.

MEDITERRANEAN SEDUCTION

From 1916, Matisse began to spend the winter months at Nice on the Riviera. Apart from the availability of many attractive Mediterranean models, the dazzling light – its play on the white stucco buildings and the clear sea – was irresistible to an artist for whom colours and light were to become a preoccupation for the next ten years. For the rest of his life, Matisse spent most of his winters in Nice – as if on sabbatical from domesticity – moving from one hotel to another, painting, rowing and playing the violin.

The peace of Matisse's life during these years is reflected in a series of quiet, contemplative interiors, such as the *Woman and Goldfish* (pp.28-9), and in his languorous odalisques (p.31). These

Two worlds meet
(right) Coptic fabrics, which combine aspects of the East and West, attracted Matisse throughout his life. He, too, created a new art from disparate heritages.

Explorer

Louvre, Paris/Réunion des Musées Nationaux

Chosen by Fate

In 1948, Matisse embarked on the most important project of his last years – the decoration of the Chapel of the Rosary in the hill-town of Vence. Matisse, himself ravaged by illness, had felt intensely sorry for an ex-model, now a Dominican nun, who had suffered from tuberculosis. Though now cured, she could no longer have children, which is why, he felt, she had entered holy orders. Persuaded by her to undertake it, he saw the project as the culmination of his life's work: 'This is not a work I chose, but rather a work for which I have been chosen by fate . . .' he said. The simple, light-flooded chapel, with its glowing colours and clear lines, epitomizes everything that Matisse was trying to achieve in his career.

A chapel of happiness

(left and below) Matisse was most concerned that the chapel should reflect light and provide a haven. He looked to mosques for inspiration, and the tall cross stands out like a beckoning minaret. Involved with every stage of the chapel's design, his most personal contribution was the design of the stained-glass windows and a series of murals painted with simple black lines on white ceramic tiles. For the windows, Matisse used a version of the paper cut-out technique he had been developing since 1937, while the murals were designed as 'the visual equivalent of a large, open book.'

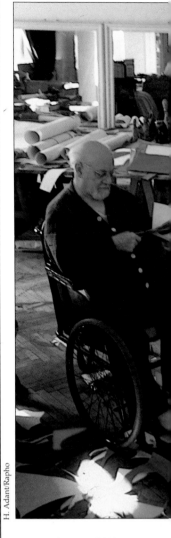

A new lease of life

(above) Confined to bed or the wheelchair, Matisse spent the last years of his life in a suite at the Hôtel Régina in Nice. Having survived two serious abdominal operations, he felt that he had been 'resurrected' from the dead, and continued working indefatigably – especially on paper cut-outs. His great preoccupation now was with light, which symbolized for him eternal life – and his last works in this gouache découpée technique were designs for stained-glass windows.

works were more acceptable to the establishment than those of his Fauvist years and from 1921, Matisse began to gain official recognition. That year, the French government purchased one of his paintings, and examples of his works began to enter major public collections all over the world. In 1925, he was created a Chevalier of the Legion of Honour. For many years, Matisse had suffered from the backlash of the Fauvist episode, which saw him branded as 'loathsome', 'abnormal' and 'degenerate'. This characterization of Matisse was entirely at odds with his true nature. He was not a passive or tranquil man and suffered continual anxiety about his art. But in his outward behaviour, he was quiet, amiable and modest. Fernande Olivier, Picasso's mistress, described him as a 'sympathetic character . . . of an astonishing lucidity of spirit, precise, concise, intelligent.' After a particularly naive response by an American interviewer, Matisse is said to have pleaded, 'Oh, do tell the American people that I am a normal man . . .'

The 1930s were years of experiment. Matisse made a trip to Tahiti via America in 1930. He denied that the trip was a flight from Western civilization and was left strangely dissatisfied by the experience. Also in 1930, Matisse undertook to provide the illustrations for a book of poems by the Symbolist poet, Mallarmé, and in 1931, he accepted the commission to provide a large-scale mural decoration for the Barnes Foundation in Philadelphia. Although the project posed monumental problems, Matisse re-worked the entire design when he learnt that he had been given incorrect measurements. Exhausted, he retreated to Italy, and revisited Giotto's murals.

In 1937, he designed the scenery and costumes for a production of Shostakovich's *Le Rouge et le Noir* by the Ballets Russes of Monte Carlo, and the following year, he began working extensively in cut paper or *gouache découpée*, a project which culminated in the publication of *Jazz* (p.19).

A SECOND LIFE

By 1939, Matisse was becoming increasingly anxious about the uncertain climate as war was about to break out. His separation from his wife, though never legalized, was pretty much on the cards. (She and Marguerite went on to work for the French Resistance and were captured by the Gestapo, though later rescued.) Matisse was seriously ill with duodenal cancer and had two major operations in 1941: surprised to find he had survived them, he felt he had been granted another life. By now, he was looked after by Lydia Delektorskaya, the young Russian model he had painted in the 1930s, who had become his muse, confidante and companion. Matisse had acquired a suite in the palatial Hôtel Régina at Nice, where he retreated to convalesce – but continued working, even from his bed: he fixed charcoal onto long poles and drew on the walls and ceiling.

As the Italians advanced on Nice, Matisse moved to the nearby hill town of Vence. It was here that he was persuaded by one of his ex-models, now a nun, to undertake the most important project of his last years – the decoration of the Chapel of the Rosary. By the time the chapel was consecrated in 1951, Matisse was too frail to attend the ceremony. Three years later, he died peacefully at Nice, on 3 November 1954, aged 84.

Confined to paradise
(left) Unable to travel anymore, Matisse created his own tropical retreat within his hotel apartment. Plants abounded and doves flew through the rooms. Looking increasingly like a venerable Oriental lord, Matisse was to end his days in a remarkable state of spiritual contentment attained through deep contemplation and his art.

© Henri Cartier-Bresson/Magnum

Balm for the Spirit

Matisse's art radiates calm and serenity. He wanted his works to induce a state of profound inner happiness, to soothe and purify the spirit and to create a sense of balance and harmony.

In a statement of 1908, Matisse explained the governing impulse behind his life's work: 'What I dream of is an art of balance, of purity and serenity devoid of troubling or disturbing subject-matter . . . like a comforting influence, a mental balm – something like a good armchair in which one rests from physical fatigue.' Throughout his career Matisse pursued this aim, the aim of evolving an art of balance and serenity, to rest and appease both the viewer and the artist himself.

In his earlier works, Matisse often chose subjects that reflected this idyllic state of being, as for example, in *Luxe, Calme et Volupté* (below) – an Arcadian vision of bathers in a light-filled landscape. As his career progressed, however, Matisse discovered that his ideal could be expressed in a less literal, more abstract way, by evoking 'feelings' or 'sensations'. He was never interested in portraying violent passions or sudden movement. Instead, he instinctively sought out subjects or forms that breathed an atmosphere of stillness and repose: languorous nudes and odalisques, interiors flooded with light and colour, and the intimate world of his studio. His models were his lifelong obsession: 'I often keep these girls for years, until my interest is exhausted', he once said. In their relaxed poses and curvaceous forms, and in his own patient method of observing them, Matisse discovered an ideal of 'sublimated voluptuousness'. He deliberately limited his range of subjects to things within his immediate experience. Often, he included sculptures in his paintings, as a reflection of his own activity as a sculptor.

Matisse achieved his aim in painting almost entirely through his use of colour. Early in his career, he discovered that colour need not be simply descriptive, but had an expressive power of its own, and could evoke particular feelings or states of mind. Matisse attributed this discovery to

Luxe, Calme et Volupté (1904)
(below) Matisse painted this vibrant image of nudes relaxing in a landscape in the divisionist style of his friend, Signac – using bright, lozenge-shaped dabs of colour. But the mechanical process of applying 'a little pink, a little blue, a little green' didn't appeal to him for long. On the other hand, the theme (inspired by a couplet from a Baudelaire poem) was to prove a lasting source of inspiration.

Artist and model
(below) Matisse observed his models in various attitudes of repose and abandonment, before deciding on the pose that best suited their nature.

Woman with Blue Eyes (1935)
(above) In the 1930s, Matisse's dominant means of expression was line-drawing, which he described as 'female' (painting being 'male'). For a while, he felt unable to reconcile the conflicting demands of the two.

Jazz (1947)
(below) The 20 stencil prints in Jazz *were created from paper cut-out designs. Matisse planned to call the book 'The Circus', but then changed the title to 'Jazz', to reflect the joyous, improvisatory nature of the imagery.*

the influence of Japanese prints, in which colour exists independently and possesses an expressive beauty of its own. Matisse gradually and persistently began to look for ways of freeing colour from its traditional naturalistic function. 'When I paint green, it doesn't mean grass; when I paint blue, it doesn't mean sky', he asserted in a famous statement. What he was looking for were colours 'to stir the sensual depths in men'.

LIVING COLOUR

Matisse's pursuit of expressive colour led him initially to the vigorous works of his Fauvist period, such as *The Open Window* (p.22). Here, the colour is no longer simply descriptive; vivid patches of vermilion, violet blue, viridian green and orange are used with little reference to the real colours of nature, as if to evoke the experience of colour itself. However, Matisse's Fauvist period was brief – the works of this time have an energy and liveliness which were ultimately foreign to his purpose. Furthermore, the separate brushstrokes of works like *The Open Window* made it difficult for Matisse to establish a clear sense of structure. After 1907, he began to work with broader, more fluid areas of paint and plainer colours in order to achieve a 'restful surface'. 'There was a time', he later wrote, 'when I never left my paintings hanging on the wall, because they reminded me of moments of nervous excitement and I did not care

Jazz: Plate II: The Circus, National Gallery of Art, Washington © DACS 1987

Odalisques

It was the French 19th-century artists Ingres and Delacroix who rediscovered the appeal of odalisques – eastern slave women imprisoned in exotic harems. Ingres never visited the East, but extracted Oriental settings for his nudes from travellers' accounts and Persian miniatures. Delacroix, however, went to North Africa and captured with great immediacy the hot-house atmosphere of the seraglio. Inspired by his example, Matisse visited Tangier and began his own series of odalisques in sumptuous interiors (p.31).

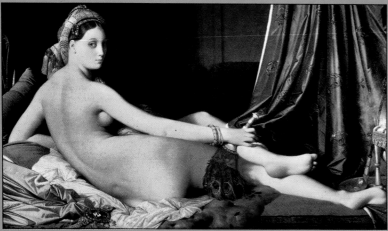

Louvre, Paris

Jean-Auguste-Dominique Ingres (1780-1867) **La Grande Odalisque** *(above) Matisse admired Ingres' 'purist' approach and the precision of his technique. He once stated that he preferred this painting to Manet's* Olympia *because 'the sensual and wilfully determined line' particularly appealed to him.*

Eugène Delacroix (1798-1863) **Women of Algiers** *(below) Delacroix visited North Africa in 1832 and made several sketches of women in an Algerian harem. He later painted them in a blaze of sensual colour, delighting in the pattern and texture of their costumes and setting.*

Louvre, Paris

to see them again when I was quiet.'

In works like *The Blue Window* (p.27) – with its radiant airy blue ground and solid patches of golden ochre – Matisse discovered the virtue of boldness. The example of Gauguin had encouraged him to use heightened colour; Gauguin had taught his students to paint a bluish shadow 'as blue as possible with pure ultramarine'. Matisse also realized that too many colours confuse the eye and lessen the impact of the preceding ones. He demanded, 'Order, above all in colour. Put three or four touches of colour, which you have understood, on the canvas; add another if you can – if you can't, set this canvas aside and begin again.'

A SENSE OF PERMANENCE

Having decided on the primacy of colour in his works, Matisse was faced with a difficult task. A strong emphasis on colour, especially when used in a non-naturalistic way, tends to accentuate the surface of the canvas, and create a predominantly decorative effect, but Matisse also wanted to give his paintings a quality of structure, depth and permanence. His most influential model in this respect was the work of Cézanne. One of Matisse's most prized possessions was a small Cézanne canvas of *Three Bathers*. When he presented the painting to the Petit Palais in 1936, Matisse wrote to the Director asking that it should be properly hung: 'It is rich in colour and surface and only when it is seen at a distance is it possible to appreciate the sweep of its lines and the exceptional sobriety of its relationships.'

Cézanne's influence is apparent both in Matisse's sculpture, and in his figure compositions, such as *Dance* (opposite) with its meticulously placed and simplified forms. But it is also evident in the gradual simplification of Matisse's work as a whole. Matisse, with his hypersensitivity to anything vaguely confusing or disquieting, learnt from the example of Cézanne that a purity and simplicity of form were essential in creating an impression of 'wholeness'. This is brilliantly achieved in works like *The Egyptian Curtain* (p.33), where bold patterns of colour and simple, solid shapes come together in a finely balanced whole. Here at last, Matisse has also come to terms with the fierceness of colour – he is no longer afraid of his fierier impulses.

Late in life, Matisse began to make paper cut-outs – his famous *gouaches découpées*. 'Cutting into living colour reminds me of the sculptor's direct carving', he explained. In these dynamic arrangements of brightly coloured shapes, Matisse triumphantly demonstrated his individual means of expression. 'Expression' does not lie 'in the passion that appears suddenly on a face or show itself in some violent movement', but it resides in the position occupied by shapes, in the empty spaces around them, in the interaction of colours and in the proportions of the whole. 'Everything', as Matisse summed up, 'has its part to play.'

LOOKING AT A MASTERPIECE

Dance

Matisse began *Dance* in 1909, for the Russian collector Sergei Shchukin, who commissioned the work as one of three panels to decorate the stairway of his palatial house in Moscow. The panel was designed to go on the first floor, and Matisse's intention was to 'summon up energy' and 'give a feeling of lightness'. The monumental figures with their pure, elastic movement, inspired by Matisse's recollection of folk-dance in Collioure, seem to convey the essence of dance, as an expression of life itself. Matisse used only three colours: the bluest of blues, brilliant green and powerful vermilion. In the evening light, the intensity of the colours made the picture 'suddenly seem to quiver and vibrate', he recalled.

TRADEMARKS

Expressive Colour

Matisse believed in the power of colour to affect the feelings, irrespective of the object it served to describe or represent. On one occasion, he used a brilliant yellow, simply 'to express excitement and pleasure at the contrast of trees and sky'. 'I think only of rendering my sensations', he wrote.

The Hermitage, Leningrad

Gallery

Matisse ranks alongside Picasso as the pre-eminent painter of the 20th century, and in the sensitivity of his line and the beauty of his colouring, he stands unrivalled among his contemporaries. Unlike many great modern artists, Matisse did not reflect in his work the troubled times through which he lived; rather he was concerned with tackling

Open Window, Collioure *1905*
21¾″ × 18½″ Whitney Collection, New York

Matisse painted this picture at Collioure, where he spent the summer of 1905 with his painter friend, André Derain. He exhibited it at the Salon d'Automne in 1905, the occasion on which he and his associates earned the nickname 'les fauves' (wild beasts). It is one of the first mature examples of a theme that was to be a favourite of Matisse's throughout his life – a fragment of a room with a view through a window. Matisse later attained grander and more sonorous effects in such works, but this one has a captivating freshness and spontaneity – a sense of joy in the handling of colour – that he rarely excelled.

aesthetic problems: 'to study separately each element of construction; drawing, colour values, composition; to explore how these elements could be combined into a synthesis without diminishing the eloquence of any one of them by the presence of the others'. His aims changed little throughout his long career, but his means became more subtle, from the inspired boldness of his Fauvist works, such as The Open Window and Madame Matisse, to the complex harmonies of Woman and Goldfish and The Egyptian Curtain. And his paper cut-outs such as La Tristesse du Roi, rank among the most glorious final testimonies an artist has ever left to the world.

Madame Matisse ('The Green Stripe') *1905* 15¾″ × 12¾″ Statens Museum for Kunst, Copenhagen

This celebrated portrait of Matisse's wife is one of the most audacious of his Fauvist works, as the use of a non-naturalistic colour in the human face is much more startling than it would be in a landscape, say, or a still-life. In spite of this bold stroke and the vigorous brushwork, the picture is much less sensuous than many of Matisse's works of this period and has a feeling of intellectual rigour about it. The green stripe, indeed, seems calculated with great care, for the powerful accent it provides stops the face being overwhelmed by the strong flat colours of the background.

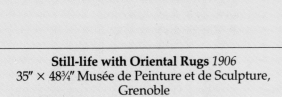

Still-life with Oriental Rugs *1906*
35″ × 48¾″ Musée de Peinture et de Sculpture,
Grenoble

Two of the themes that were to be recurring features in Matisse's work appear in this painting – an interest in textiles and a fascination with the exotic beauty of the Orient. He came from an area where weaving was a traditional craft, and around the time this picture was painted he frequented the shop of a Lebanese rug dealer in Paris. Matisse clearly relishes painting the variegated colours and shapes of the rugs and it is characteristic of his work that he is much more interested in the surface pattern his picture creates than in representing a realistic sense of space and depth.

Goldfish and Sculpture *(1911)*
46″ × 39⅝″; oil on canvas.
Collection, The Museum of Modern Art, New York

*A piece of sculpture is a prominent motif in several of Matisse's works
of this period, and often it is similar in form to his own sculpture.
Here, Matisse unerringly combines disarmingly simple and direct
draughtsmanship with lush expanses of decorative colour.*

The Blue Window *(1911, autumn)*
51½″ × 35⅝″; oil on canvas.
Collection, The Museum of Modern Art, New York

This is a view from the bedroom of Matisse and his wife in their villa at Issy-les-Molineaux. The roof of Matisse's studio can be seen emerging through the trees at the left. Here, in his love of colour, Matisse abandons its descriptive function in favour of its evocative qualities.

Woman and Goldfish *1921*
31½″ × 39″ Art Institute of Chicago

A goldfish bowl is a favourite theme in Matisse's paintings, but this picture is unusual for him in its sense of three-dimensional solidity and in its air of rapt concentration. The woman's pensive pose and expression are rendered with masterly economy, and the comparatively subdued and dense colouring of pink, brown and gentle blue-green adds to the soporific atmosphere, as if she is drifting into a deep day-dream.

Two Women in an Interior 1920
18¼″ × 25¾″ Musée de l'Annonciade

From the early 1920s, Matisse spent much of his time on the Riviera. The bright light of the South of France that appealed so strongly to him is apparent even in this quiet interior. The sitters are Matisse's daughter and Mademoiselle Daricaret.

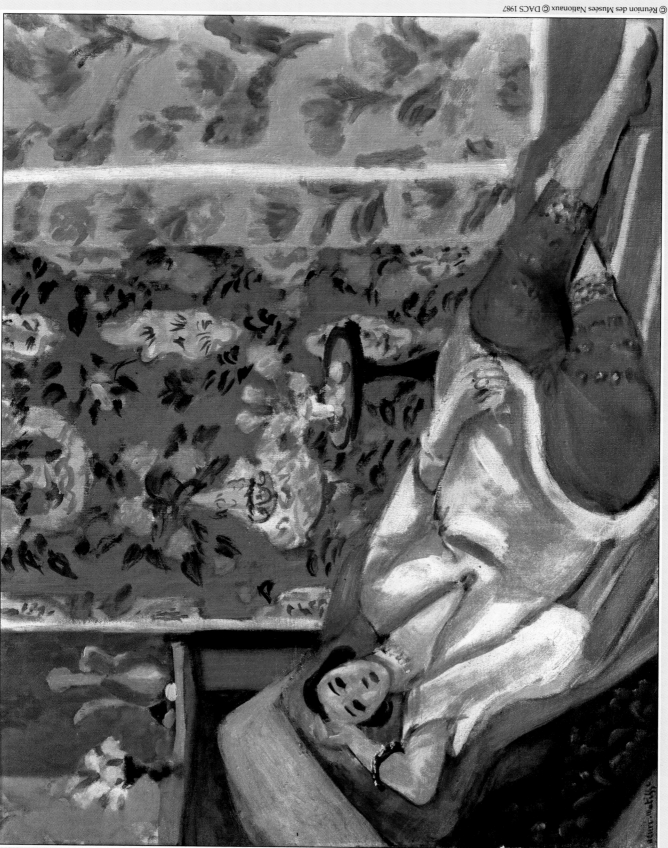

Odalisque with Red Bloomers c.1924-25
19¾″ × 24″ Musée National d'Art Moderne, Paris

The odalisque was a theme that Matisse made his own. In some of his representations of the subject he concentrates on the formal qualities of the figure, but here he gives himself over entirely to the sensuality appropriate to the theme, particularly in the background.

Red Interior, Still-life on a Blue Table *1947*
45½″ × 35″ Kunstsammlung Nordrhein-Westfalen, Düsseldorf

*In 1947-48, Matisse painted a remarkable series of interiors that his
secretary justifiably described as 'dazzling'; this picture and the one on
the opposite page are two of the finest examples. They show astonishing
creative energy for a man in his late 70s, and here the bold contrasts of
red and blue and the leaping black zigzags create a feeling of vibrancy.*

The Egyptian Curtain *1948*
45½″ × 35″ The Phillips Collection, Washington

*This is perhaps the greatest of all Matisse's paintings on the theme of
the view through a window and one of his most brilliant demonstrations
of understanding of light. The heavy, earthy red and black forms of the
curtain provide the perfect foil for the palm tree, which seems almost to
explode in a shower of yellow and green.*

Henri Matisse

La Tristesse du Roi (Sorrow of the King)
1952
115″ × 156″ Musée National d'Art Moderne, Paris

From the early 1940s, Matisse, confined to a wheelchair, worked in the medium called gouache découpée (paper cut-outs), of which this is one of the most majestic examples. Assistants working under his direction pinned the pieces of cut-out coloured paper to the background sheet, and when Matisse was satisfied with the arrangement they were pasted into place. The pictures thus created must rank among the most joyous and original works ever made by an artist in old age. 'The paper cut-out', he said, 'allows me to draw in the colour. It is a simplification for me. Instead of drawing the outline and putting the colour inside it – the one modifying the other – I draw straight into the colour.' The colours themselves were often so dazzling that Matisse's doctor advised him to wear dark glasses. Some of the designs are purely abstract, but here there are figural suggestions, and Matisse may have been inspired by a Rembrandt painting of Saul and David, in which the young David attempts to soothe the troubled King Saul with his music-making. Here it is the king figure himself who holds what is clearly a guitar-like instrument.

The Lure of the South

The South of France, with its brilliant light, deep shadows and bright colours, began to attract artists away from Paris in the summer during the 1880s. Some, like Renoir, settled there.

Long before sunbathing became fashionable in the 1920s, artists had discovered the attractions of resorts in the South of France. Paul Signac, for instance, sailed into St Tropez in 1892, when it was still a humble fishing village dependent for trade and communication on the sea. He admired not only the deep cobalt blue of the Mediterranean, but also the stalwart fisherfolk who 'wrested a painful living from its depths'.

It was in the 1880s, that artists like Van Gogh and Cézanne began to appreciate the special light of the South, which became the main attraction for subsequent generations of painters. So different from the diffuse, grey light of Paris and the North, the brilliant Mediterranean sun sharpened contrasts and flattened objects, and its intensity brought home to them the impossibility of imitating nature exactly in their canvases. 'Sunlight cannot be reproduced', Cézanne remarked to Maurice Denis, 'it must be represented by something else . . . by colour'. Van Gogh found the same problem in Saintes-Maries-sur-Mer in 1888, and wrote to his brother Theo: 'Now that I have seen the sea here I feel how

important it is to stay in the South, and also feel how I must intensify my colour.'

This brilliant light sharpened the colour contrasts between the deep blue of the Mediterranean, the orange-reds of the village roofs, the rocky outcrops and the sandstone soil, and the dark greens and purples of a landscape dotted with olive groves, pines and cypresses. The dramatic and colourful coastline provided panoramic views, as well as a wealth of individual motifs, and Renoir found it a relief from what he called the 'absurd lacework' of the cliffs lining the Normandy coast. He settled permanently in the South in 1907, but two decades earlier he had spent a winter exploring the Côte from Marseilles to Genoa with Monet. Monet was so taken by the southern scenery that he immediately planned a return visit alone to work, and cautioned his dealer Durand Ruel to keep it secret: 'If Renoir knew I was just about to go off, he would undoubtedly want to come with me and each of us would be a bad influence on the other'.

Many painters followed this pattern of winter trips to the South, where the light was still

Southern light
(left) Attracted by the sparkling light of the South, artists regularly began to visit the little-known Côte d'Azur.

Cézanne in Provence
(right) Cézanne lived for a while in L'Estaque, a small fishing village near Marseille, where this landscape was painted. While working in the hills above L'Estaque, Cézanne would discard paintings with which he was dissatisfied and it was here that Renoir stumbled upon a Cézanne watercolour of Bathers.

Brigitte and Jose Dupont © Explorer

Cézanne: Estaque from the Gulf of Marseilles. Paris, Musée d'Orsay/Giraudon

The painter on his way to work

(left) Van Gogh's move to Arles, inspired by the light, encouraged him to intensify his colours. Full of enthusiasm, he wrote, 'I have faith that a new school of colourists will take root in the Midi'. This painting shows him going off to work in the open air.

Renoir at 'Les Collettes'

(right) In middle age, Renoir began to suffer from arthritis, which eventually crippled him. He moved permanently to the warmer climate of the South of France in 1907, where he built his house 'Les Collettes' at Cagnes. Here he lived out his last years still painting, but from a wheelchair with a brush strapped to his twisted hand.

Roger-Viollet

Van Gogh: The Road to Tarascon

remarkably constant, but some, like Signac, preferred to establish a permanent base there. When Signac arrived in St Tropez, it was still inaccessible except by sea, and he was immediately enchanted by the cluster of white, pink and yellow houses, the picturesque aspect of the harbour and its traffic, and the dramatic violet of the sea under the peculiar light of St Tropez, caused by the northern aspect of the peninsula.

ARTISTS COLONY AT ST TROPEZ

He bought a villa – La Hune – overlooking the harbour, where he entertained friends when he was not painting, 'talking tides' with the fishermen, or cruising in one of his many yachts. Henri-Edmond Cross, another important Neo-Impressionist painter, lived in the neighbouring village of Le Lavandou, and used to pay frequent visits to La Hune, and in 1904 Matisse went to spend the summer months there.

Matisse's favourite local motif was the broken coastline of the gulf seen from the end of a pine grove, which he painted over and over again using an electric rainbow palette and the divisionist technique of Signac and Cross. *Luxe, Calme et Volupté* (p.18) – the most famous of these views – was exhibited at the October 1904 Salon d'Automne in Paris, and caused an immediate exodus to the South. 'They all went down there', Louis Vauxcelles remembered, 'like a flock of

Explorer

Jean-Loup Charmet

Signac at St Tropez

Signac settled in St Tropez (above) in 1892. There his technique developed, his colouring becoming bolder and his 'pointillist' dots larger, to form a mosaic pattern, as in Entrance to the Port of St Tropez *(right). He invited Matisse to stay with him in 1904, and the visit inspired Matisse's* Luxe, Calme et Volupté *set on the shores of St Tropez. Signac liked the painting so much that he bought it for his villa in the town.*

migratory birds. By the spring of 1905, there was a valiant little colony of painters painting and arguing in this enchanted region: Signac, Cross, Manguin, Camoin, Marquet . . . '

The Fauve Henri Manguin was a flamboyant addition to St Tropez dressed in his velvet gaiters, flowing cravat and broad-brimmed hat. He bought a studio, 'L'Oustalet', overlooking the bay, where he lived until it was destroyed by the Germans in 1944; and Charles Camoin could still be found painting in the 1960s on the Quai Jean Jaurès, until the start of the tourist season each year.

In 1905, Matisse and Derain spent the summer in Collioure, then a small Catalan seaport of Perpignan and just a few miles from the Spanish border. The colourful boats and the squat houses rising from the sea to the foothills of the Pyrenees were the subjects of their first 'Fauve' pictures, vibrant with hot and sensuous colours, and painted without shadows. Away from the social life of Paris there were few distractions and although the pace was slow in the South, Matisse proved a demanding companion. 'I don't mind telling you', Derain wrote to Vlaminck, 'its no fun at all, but I'm staying on because here I'm compelled to buckle down to work seriously and put my heart in it . . .' For the next ten years

Private Collection, Paris. Photo: Lauros-Giraudon © DACS 1987

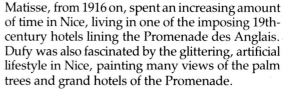

76 NICE - Hôtel Ruhl et Promenade des Anglais. RM

Matisse, from 1916 on, spent an increasing amount of time in Nice, living in one of the imposing 19th-century hotels lining the Promenade des Anglais. Dufy was also fascinated by the glittering, artificial lifestyle in Nice, painting many views of the palm trees and grand hotels of the Promenade.

After the Second World War, Picasso settled first at Antibes, where he worked in the Chateau Grimaldi, then at Vallauris, where he breathed new life into the dying ceramic industry, and finally as a recluse in his villa at Cannes, 'La Californie'. Chagall, too, had moved south, into a villa at Vence, secluded among orange groves and eucalyptus trees, which had previously been let to a painter who faked Matisses. Ironically, the grand old man himself was living closeby in Cumiez, a residential suburb of Nice.

The works of Cézanne and Picasso, Matisse and the Fauves and the prismatic watercolours of Dufy were the most effective of advertising brochures for the South of France. But as the artists discovered the South of France, so did the tourists, and it gradually became the thriving holiday centre it is today. What remains of the artists there is to be found in the museums devoted to them which exist throughout the Côte d'Azur.

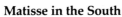

Matisse in the South
From 1916, Matisse (right) spent his winters in Nice, staying in one of the hotels on the palm-fringed Promenade des Anglais (above), until he acquired a flat in the old part of Nice in 1921. Here, he painted many of his sunny Nice interiors, concentrating on the effect of light flooding through the window. He later moved to the Hôtel Régina where the ironwork balcony of his room featured in many of his works.

Matisse returned to Collioure in the summer.

Renoir, meanwhile, had settled in Cagnes-sur-Mer, hopeful that the sun and the heat would ease his chronic rheumatoid arthritis. One of the earliest 'environmentalists', he bought a plot of land at Les Collettes to save some ancient threatened olive trees, believed to have been 1000 years old. Halfway up the hill and secluded amongst the olive groves, he built a house where he spent the last years of his life eventually confined to a wheelchair, his hands so distorted that they had to be bandaged to prevent his fingernails from digging in. But he painted cheerfully on, while friends and dealers paid frequent visits, including the apish Creole Ambroise Vollard, who made an amusing spectacle swinging from a tree in Renoir's garden. 'My dear Vollard', Renoir would remind him, 'that is not a coconut palm'.

RETREAT TO THE SOUTH

Apart from the climate and the artistic potential of the South, the resorts provided respite from the horrors of both world wars and from Nazi persecution. Picasso made frequent trips to Provence and especially the Riviera, while

Henri Cartier-Bresson © John Hillelson Agency

A Year in the Life 1951

The completion of Matisse's chapel at Vence was, like the Festival of Britain, a bright spot on the still war-torn landscape of Europe. In 1951, the Common Market was foreshadowed by the Iron and Steel Community, and the West, already part of a military bloc, was locked in a Cold War that had boiled over in Korea.

Matisse's continuing achievement, and the thought-provoking work of writers such as Sartre and Camus, proved that French culture was still a creative force. However, France's political instability – there were three ministries in 1951 alone – highlighted the weaknesses of the Fourth Republic. At the time, these seemed more significant than the initiatives that had been taken by French Foreign Minister Robert Schuman, whose plan for an iron and steel customs union in western Europe was being put into its final shape, ready for implementation in 1952. Britain declined to participate in the Schuman Plan, and in so doing, failed to foresee the importance of the Iron and Steel Community or its wider-ranging successor, the Common Market.

After years of war and austerity, things looked up in Britain

당과 수령께 무한히 충직한 혁명

National festivities

(above) Originally organized to commemorate the Great Exhibition of 1851, the Festival of Britain was more of an attempt at national jollification after the rigours of the war and its aftermath than an exhibition per se. The London site for the Festival on the South Bank of the Thames was soon covered with extraordinary buildings such as the Skylon and the Dome of Discovery. More permanent constructions were the London Festival Hall and further down river, the funfair and gardens of Battersea park, here illuminated by fireworks. Nor was the Festival limited to London; local committees throughout the country organized their own festivities.

in the summer of 1951. To commemorate the hundredth anniversary of the 1851 Great Exhibition – itself a celebration of Britain's 19th-century industrial supremacy – the Festival of Britain was launched after several years of preparation. Pageants, exhibitions and arts festivals were held all over the country; one of them, the Edinburgh Festival, was to become a regular feature of the British cultural life. The heart of the Festival of Britain was the blitzed south bank of the River Thames in London, where eight and a half million people visited the pavilions devoted to Britain and the British way of life. The most striking landmarks were the huge Dome of Discovery, the monumental, javelin-like Skylon, and a single permanent building, the Royal Festival Hall.

The Festival of Britian was the last major achievement of the

Labour government led by Clement Attlee. In the months before Labour's defeat in October 1951, Aneurin Bevan and Harold Wilson resigned from the Cabinet in protest against increased National Health prescription charges. The new charges were largely necessitated by the massive rearmament programme which had been embarked upon in 1950.

THE COLD WAR

The intensification of the Cold War between East and West – and its 'hot' accompaniment in Korea – determined many decisions made in 1950-51, including the rearmament of West Germany and her early reintegration into the economic and security systems of western Europe. The pre-war intellectual

Lakeshore Drive Apartments
(below) The German architect Ludwig Mies van der Rohe (1886-1969) had by the early 1920s become a leading exponent of modern architecture. In 1933, he resigned from his directorship of the Bauhaus when the political trends of Nazism became self-evident, emigrating to the United States five years later. His apartments at 860-880 Lakeshore Drive, Chicago (1948-51) reflect his dictum that true architecture stems from the needs and means of the times rather than from personal expression. These two anonymous glass tower blocks, astonishing at the time, were the prototype of the modern tower block which is so familiar to us today.

The war in Korea
(left) By the end of 1950, the American and UN thrust into North Korea had been pushed back; a huge Chinese army had entered the conflict in support of their Communist neighbour. Seoul, capital of South Korea, fell once again to the Communists, but they in turn were brought to a halt by a determined counter-offensive early in 1951 and forced back beyond the 38th parallel. Peace talks began, but an armistice was not signed until July 1953. This poster shows General Kim Il Sung, Commander-in-Chief of the Communist forces.

MacArthur dismissed
(above) General MacArthur, Commander-in-Chief of the UN and US army in Korea, had been urging the American government to take the war into mainland China with the aid of Nationalist Chinese troops. His public statement of disagreement with President Truman's policy of containment led to his peremptory dismissal in April 1951. Pictured here at a press conference on his return to the US for the first time in 14 years, the General was given a hero's welcome.

vogue of Communism disappeared, though some faithful believers remained undetected in high places. In May 1951, two diplomats facing exposure – Guy Burgess and Donald Maclean – defected to Moscow.

Bitter fighting went on in Korea throughout the year. Although there were a number of dramatic incidents, it became apparent that the battlelines had more or less stabilized along the 38th parallel. Several unsuccessful overtures were made to arrange a truce. Frustrated by the United States' inability to win the war, General Douglas MacArthur pressed for action against the North Koreans' Chinese allies, despite the danger of spreading the war. When President Truman refused, MacArthur publicly criticized the administration, perhaps believing that his great prestige from the Second World War made him invulnerable. Nevertheless, Truman relieved him of his command, and his career came to an end.

During 1951, Dr Mussadeq became Prime Minister of Iran and outraged Britain by nationalizing the Anglo-Iranian Oil Company. Libya, not yet oil-rich, became independent under King Idris I. Abdullah of Jordan was assassinated and Syria experienced her fourth military coup in less than three years. Britten's *Billy Budd* and Stravinsky's *Rake's Progress* received their first performances. Three longtime best-selling novels were published: Nicholas Monsarrat's *The Cruel Sea*, J. D. Salinger's *Catcher in the Rye* and Herman Wouk's *The Caine Mutiny*. And, in Britain's cinemas, the 'H' (for horror) certificate was replaced by a new sex-and-horror rating: the 'X-film' reached the screens.

The African Queen (1951)

(right) John Huston's celebrated film, set in West Africa, tells the story of the development of an unlikely love affair between a rough Canadian engineer and a prim Methodist missionary, forced to escape the Germans at the outbreak of World War I in the dilapidated boat of the title. Humphrey Bogart won an Oscar for Best Actor and Katherine Hepburn just missed one, despite one of the most dramatic screen performances of her entire career.

Spy scandal

(below) Guy Burgess and Donald Maclean, two British diplomats with Communist sympathies and acquainted since students days at Cambridge, disappeared on 25 May 1951. Only five years later did the Soviets publicly acknowledge that the two agents had defected. The British Security Services, who had been ineptly trailing Maclean under suspicion of giving away atomic secrets, had only themselves to blame. Burgess, via a 'third man', Kim Philby who was to defect later, tipped off Maclean. This photograph of 1956 shows Burgess relaxing by the Black Sea.

Kobal Collection

Popperfoto

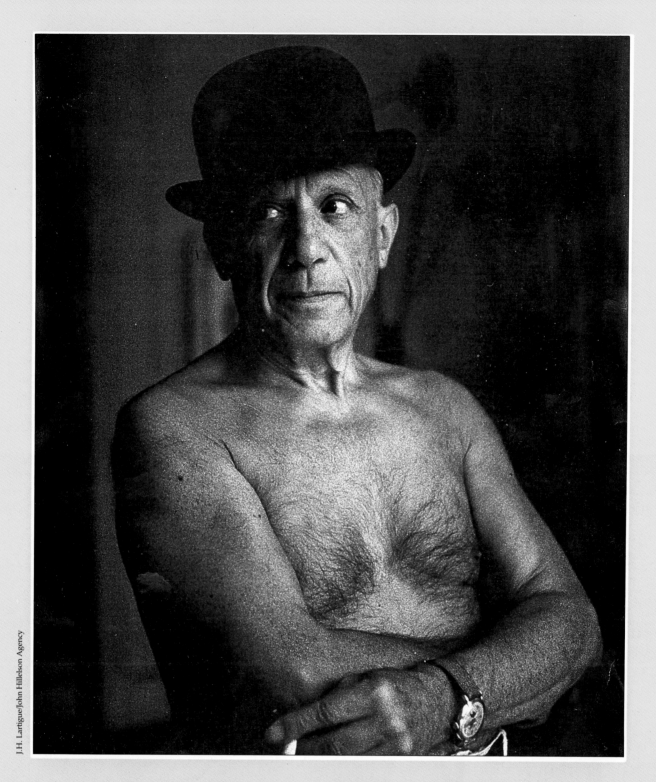

PABLO PICASSO

1881-1973

Picasso is a legendary figure, the most famous and the most profoundly original artist this century has produced. Sensual and charismatic, his turbulent love-life was the springboard of his art. He was fond of calling women 'goddesses or doormats', but they were his greatest source of inspiration. He dominated the artistic avant-garde up until the Second World War, and few artists escaped his influence.

Picasso's inventive brilliance encompassed many different styles and media, but perhaps his most significant contribution was the development of Cubism, which paved the way for the abstract art of recent decades. Although his direct influence declined after 1945, Picasso continued to work compulsively through the 50s and 60s. Since his death at the age of 91, his reputation has remained unchallenged.

The Genius of Modern Art

An infant prodigy, Picasso became the most influential artist of the 20th century. His long life was dominated by a series of emotional attachments which helped to shape the direction of his art.

Pablo Ruiz Picasso was born in Plaza de la Merced, Málaga, Spain, on 25 October 1881. It was a difficult birth, and the baby apparently had cigar smoke blown up his nostrils to force his first few breaths in the world. Picasso was the only boy in the family, and with his good looks and precocious talent, was soon used to the adulation and love which accompanied him throughout his life.

Picasso's father, José Ruiz Blasco was also an artist – dead game still-lifes and bunches of lilac were his forte – but for a living he taught drawing and was the curator of the local museum. Both Don José and Picasso's mother, María Picasso López, encouraged their son's artistic ambitions as they recognized his outstanding talent at a very early age. Picasso later adopted his mother's name, as 'Ruiz' was common in the area.

Picasso never wanted to do anything but paint, and would refuse to stay at school unless he could keep one of his father's pigeons and some paintbrushes with him. Don José encouraged Picasso to draw in the academic discipline; much later, as an old man studying an exhibition of children's drawings, Picasso remarked, 'When I was their age I could draw like Raphael, but it took me a lifetime to learn to draw like them.'

In 1895, the family moved to Barcelona, then a literary and artistic centre receptive to the ideas of

The young Picasso
(above) Picasso was an intelligent and profoundly sensitive boy. His pale face was dominated by dark eyes which friends said were 'embarrassing in their intensity.'

A precocious talent
(right) Picasso's early drawings and portraits demonstrate his technical virtuosity and maturity. This exquisite pastel of his mother was drawn when he was only 15.

other artists in the galleries of the Rue Lafitte.

Every avant-garde style could be seen in Paris, and Picasso quickly assimilated the fundamentals of each. In the evenings he would search out Toulouse-Lautrec's subjects in the cafés and brothels of Montmartre. He met the poet and journalist, Max Jacob, who was to be a lifelong friend. In spite of Picasso's poor grasp of French, Max Jacob opened the artist's ears to the poetry of Baudelaire, Rimbaud, Verlaine and Mallarmé. Many of Picasso's most intimate friends were subsequently to be poets.

Picasso and Max Jacob lived together, sharing a bed which Max used by night and Picasso by day (his normal practice was to work at night). It was a period of extreme poverty, cold and despair. Bundles of Picasso's drawings were burnt for warmth. Picasso was also deeply depressed by the suicide of an old friend, Carlos Casagemas, due to an unhappy love affair. All these trials and sufferings were put into the haunting pictures of the Blue period (1901-4/5) – Picasso's first really independent style – when he used social outcasts as his subjects to paint the themes of poverty, blindness, alienation and despair in cold tones of

Key Dates

1881 born in Málaga, Spain

1895 moves to Barcelona; enters La Lonja Academy

1900 travels to Paris

1904 meets Fernande Olivier

1907 paints *Les Demoiselles d'Avignon*; starts developing Cubism

1912 falls in love with Marcelle Humbert ('Eva')

1917 travels to Rome to design *Parade*; meets Olga Koklova

1918 marries Olga

1925 paints *The Three Dancers*

1927 starts affair with Marie-Thérèse Walter

1935 separates from Olga

1936 meets Dora Maar; Spanish Civil War

1937 paints *Guernica*

1943 meets Françoise Gilot

1961 marries Jacqueline Roque

1973 dies at Mougins, France

Ties with Spain
(above) The artist spent his youth in Málaga and Barcelona and was fiercely proud of his origins. Throughout his life he remained deeply involved in his country's plight.

Success in Paris
(right) In 1900, Picasso travelled to Paris to broaden his horizons. He settled permanently in Montmartre in 1904 and soon established himself in artistic circles.

the European avant-garde. Although he was put into the advanced classes at the Academy of La Lonja and produced a series of traditional portraits and large figure compositions, Picasso soon broke with the academic tradition. This was helped by eight months of sketching, working and eating with the peasants of the primitive village of Horta de San Juan in Catalonia, where he recuperated after scarlet fever in spring 1898.

A STIMULATING ENVIRONMENT

Picasso thrived on the intellectual and bohemian atmosphere of the city of Barcelona. Writers, poets, journalists and artists would meet at Els Quatre Gats, a café with the distinctive flavour of the Parisian Latin Quarter. Late at night, after their philosophical and artistic discussions, Picasso and his friends would visit the music hall and the prostitutes of the Bario Chino, Barcelona's lively red light district.

In spite of what Barcelona offered, every aspiring artist had to make his way to Paris, the cultural centre of the avant-garde at the turn of the century. Picasso arrived there in 1900 and spent the next three years alternating between Paris and Barcelona. Days were spent studying the Greek, Roman and Egyptian rooms at the Louvre, and the works of Bonnard, Denis, Toulouse-Lautrec and

'Parade'

In 1916, Jean Cocteau asked Picasso to design the décor and costumes for a ballet he had written, based on scenes of popular circus life on the Parisian boulevards. It was to be produced by Serge Diaghilev, whose exotic Ballets Russes had taken Paris by storm since 1909. Cocteau and Picasso travelled to Rome in 1917 to meet Diaghilev, and Picasso took a studio on the Via Margutta. He worked very hard by day, designing costumes for a Chinese conjurer, a little American girl, two acrobats, and three stage managers (who were to stamp around on stage wearing bizarre 10ft-high Cubist constructions), and enjoyed himself by night. Back in Paris, Picasso painted the drop-curtain. *Parade* opened in Paris on 18 May 1917, and was greeted by shouts of 'sales Boches' ('dirty Jerries' – the worst wartime insult). It was revived, however, with enormous success, in 1920.

Popperfoto

Picasso's first wife
(above) While in Rome, Picasso met Olga Koklova, one of Diaghilev's dancers. The daughter of a Russian general, Olga was beautiful, strong-willed, and conventional. The couple are seen here at the opening of Parade in Paris in May 1917; they were married a year later.

© DACS 1987

Musée National d'Art Moderne, Georges Pompidou Centre, Paris

The drop-curtain
(left) Picasso's drop-curtain shows the harlequins and circus folk who appeared in his paintings of the Rose period. But here the colours are stronger, and the curtain has the appearance of a striking circus poster, which the audience understood and applauded.

cobalt and indigo.

It took a statuesque and beautiful woman to banish the starving figures of the Blue period from Picasso's work. She was Fernande Olivier, Picasso's first lasting attachment. The Rose period paintings of 1905-6, with their graceful serenity and sensuality, were the result of this new feeling of security. Picasso was working very hard at night, going to bed at dawn and getting up for a bath and breakfast at 4 pm. His new subjects were acrobats and dancers, romantic harlequins (self-portraits) and other circus artists, inspired by the characters of the Medrano circus which he often visited with Fernande.

Friends and cohabitants who gathered at the Bateau-Lavoir on the Butte de Montmartre included the artists Gris, Derain, Vlaminck, Matisse and Braque, with whom Picasso developed the concept of Cubism; the critics Guillaume Apollinaire and André Salmon, together with the collectors Gertrude and Leo Stein who regularly bought from Picasso, and several dealers including, by 1907, Daniel-Henry Kahnweiler. The paintings of the Rose period sold very well – soon Picasso's days of poverty were over for good.

In 1907, Picasso painted *Les Demoiselles d'Avignon* (pp.56-7), depicting figures in a brothel. He had been working towards a less naturalistic, more geometrical style, and had also discovered the savage Negro and Polynesian sculpture which could be found in a few shops in Paris, and which

Luc Jourbet, Paris

Model and mistress
(above) Picasso's affair with Marie-Thérèse began after he saw her on the street and said 'you have an interesting face. I would like to make your portrait'.

Robert Capa/Magnum/John Hillelson Agency Ltd

encouraged him to use totem figures and masks in his paintings. *Les Demoiselles d'Avignon* shocked even his closest friends, including Braque, but Braque was drawn to Picasso's innovations.

The burst of creative energy which produced Picasso's Cubist paintings had been released by Marcelle Humbert, a new woman in his life whom he rechristened 'Eva' – his 'first love'. His relationship with Fernande had become increasingly strained, and came to an abrupt end in the spring of 1912 when he took Eva to Avignon.

Braque and Picasso would now work together in Paris during the winter, and in the country during the summer, but the outbreak of war in 1914 halted their fruitful partnership. Braque enlisted, but Picasso, as a Spaniard in France and a pacifist, did not. Other friends, including Apollinaire and Derain also enlisted, and Picasso felt increasingly isolated and depressed, finding it difficult to work. His loneliness was compounded by the death of Eva from tuberculosis in 1915.

Picasso was saved, in 1917, by Jean Cocteau, who took him to Rome to design the backdrop, scenery and costumes for *Parade*, a ballet that Diaghilev was putting on with the Ballets Russes. There Picasso studied Michelangelo and Raphael in the Vatican and the Sistine Chapel, and also fell in love with Olga Koklova, a member of Diaghilev's corps de ballet.

Olga and Picasso were married on 12 July 1918. With her encouragement, Picasso became a society artist and launched himself into 'la vie snob', moving into a grand apartment on Rue la Boëtie – a desirable area of Paris. He was fêted by all the socialites and became the fashionable focus of every salon, gradually losing touch with his old bohemian friends.

Although the opening night of *Parade* had been a dramatic flop, Picasso continued to work with Diaghilev until 1924. At the same time he was producing Cubist landscapes and still-lifes and, when Olga became pregnant, a series of mother and child paintings and voluptuous nudes. Their son, Paulo, was born on 4 February 1921.

Throughout the 1920s and 1930s, Picasso continued to paint in alternating styles. He was aware of the new developments in modern art –

Happy years
(above) Françoise Gilot was a promising painter whom Picasso first met in May 1943. Intelligent, vivacious and beautiful, she saw her relationship with Picasso as 'a challenge I could not turn down'. She began to live with him in 1946 and brought a period of happiness and stability, delighting Picasso with the births of Claude and Paloma.

47

Surrealism, Expressionism, and abstract painting – and in 1923 had been claimed by André Breton as an initiator of Surrealism, but he was fundamentally opposed to the Surrealist use of the irrational and the subconscious. Nothing distracted him from his search for new means of expressing the human condition and the human form. The *Three Dancers* (pp.50-51) was the first of his paintings to show violent emotion and distortion of the figure. These human 'monsters' continued to appear throughout the late 20s and 30s.

This has been partly blamed on Picasso's failing marriage. Picasso had grown increasingly dissatisfied with his lifestyle, and Olga had become irritable and jealous. He shut himself away in the studio to escape the problems, working on engravings for Ovid's *Metamorphoses* and Balzac's *Chef d'Oeuvre Inconnu*. Olga's jealousy found an outlet when Picasso started an affair with the tall, blond 17-year-old Marie-Thérèse Walter in 1927, and their marriage finally broke up when Marie-Thérèse became pregnant in 1935, and Picasso asked for a divorce. Still officially a Spanish citizen,

he could only obtain a legal separation. Olga, however, remained in the background of his life until her own death from cancer in 1955. She wrote him lengthy, abusive letters almost every day and would turn up at exhibitions or on the beach, anywhere she knew she would find him, to scream insults at him and his female companions.

COMPLICATED RELATIONSHIPS

No sooner had Marie-Thérèse given birth to a girl, Maia, and Picasso had settled back into his bohemian lifestyle, than he found a new love in Dora Maar, a photographer and friend of the poet Paul Eluard. Dora provided intellectual stimulation for him, while Marie-Thérèse gave him physical satisfaction. The two women loathed each other, but apparently Picasso rather enjoyed the turbulent scenes between them. Dora was a temperamental depressive, however, and their relationship was destined to be stormy. From 1936 onwards, it was she whom Picasso subjected to the most violent distortions in his paintings.

Spanish Civil War

In 1936, the vicious antagonism between the Spanish right wing and the left-wing Republicans who won the general election that year exploded into civil war. General Franco, with the army and the aristocracy behind him, led a military uprising which threw Spain into two-and-a-half years of bloody confrontation and chaos. Picasso felt for the sufferings of his people, and, though a pacifist, he produced a satirical leaflet, *The Dream and Lie of Franco*, which was sold to raise funds for needy Republicans. His ultimate expression of the horror of the war was the painting *Guernica* (pp.64-5).

Bloody battles
(below) The civil war was exceptionally brutal; the government militia and the Republicans fought battles on the streets, churches were burnt to the ground and thousands killed.

Foreign solidarity
(right) The left-wing cause inspired international sympathy. Posters such as this called for solidarity with the Spanish workers struggling to preserve their Republic.

Poster by Barras Casanova/Lords Gallery Ltd, London

In 1936, civil war broke out in Spain, and Picasso, always on the side of the people, supported the Republican Government against Franco's military uprising. He was appointed Director of the Prado, and the Government commissioned a mural for the Spanish Pavilion at the International Exhibition in Paris. On 26 April 1937, Nazi bombers in Franco's pay left the little town of Guernica in the Basque region razed to the ground, with 2000 dead and thousands more wounded. Picasso took this outrageous crime as his subject for the commission, painting the 25ft x 11ft *Guernica* (pp.64-5) in only a month.

During the occupation a few years later, Picasso would give Nazis visiting his studio a photograph of *Guernica* as a memento. But although they regarded his art as degenerate, they gave him relatively little trouble during the war, which he spent at first in Royan and then in Paris. In 1943, Picasso met the graceful 21-year-old Françoise Gilot. Their relationship aggravated Dora's disturbed mental state, prompting a breakdown.

With Françoise, Picasso found a temporary

Untiring genius
(left) Much of Picasso's success lay in his endless creativity and versatility. This photograph shows the artist at Cannes in 1960 with one of his sculptures.

A doting father
(above) The ageing Picasso helps Paloma and Claude to draw. He once remarked that it had taken him a lifetime to learn to draw like a child.

period of security which inspired the *Joie de Vivre* paintings of dancing nymphs, satyrs and centaurs. They settled after the war first at Antibes, and then at La Galloise villa in Vallauris, where Picasso took up pottery. His fame helped to re-establish Vallauris as a centre of the ceramic industry. Françoise, however, hated the lack of privacy there. Two children, Claude (born in 1947) and Paloma (born in 1949), did not succeed in keeping their relationship alive, and in 1953 Françoise eventually left. She reappeared briefly in 1954, only to find that Jacqueline Roque had already taken her place. Picasso married Jacqueline in March 1961 at Vallauris.

Jacqueline created a peaceful atmosphere for Picasso's final years. His work during the 1950s and 60s, although still technically admirable and produced in great quantities, declined somewhat in imaginative power. He started several series of variations on old masterpieces: *Les Femmes d'Algers* by Delacroix, Velázquez's *Las Meninas*, and Manet's *Déjeuner sur l'Herbe*. His deliberate attachment to Velázquez and Manet reveals how far he had retreated from the avant-garde.

At Notre Dame de Vie, their last shared house, Picasso became virtually a recluse, although no less of a legend for it. Eventually, a prostate and gall bladder operation and failing eyesight halted his painting, and he died on 8 April 1973. His position as the most influential painter of the 20th century is still unchallenged.

New Ways of Seeing

Picasso's fertile imagination, extraordinary natural ability and endless versatility led to the exploration of new modes of expression which were to shape the course of modern art.

Picasso's output was prodigious. In his early years in Paris he was rumoured to be painting three canvases a day. He certainly could work incredibly quickly, and in his 70s and 80s was still painting with the same sense of urgency. He also tackled every imaginable medium: oil, ink, crayon, pencil, charcoal, sculpture with iron, bronze, plaster, sheet metal, stone, constructions with bric-à-brac pulled out of dustbins, engravings, lithographs — the list is endless. As an old man Picasso took up ceramics and revolutionized the techniques of linocutting. Work for Picasso was a way of life.

The styles Picasso worked in are equally varied, and he never meant his artistic output to be viewed in the light of progression or development. For much of his life he worked simultaneously in many different styles, choosing the one which suited the mood of the moment, and which could best express that mood. He could switch instantly from a Cubist construction to a classical line drawing. 'The several manners I have used in my art,' Picasso said, 'must not be considered as an evolution, or as steps toward an unknown ideal of painting. When I have found something to express, I have done it without thinking of the past or of the future. I do not believe I have used radically different elements in the different

manners I have used in painting. If the subjects I have wanted to express have suggested different ways of expression, I haven't hesitated to adopt them. I have never experimented.'

EMOTIONAL INVOLVEMENT

Picasso was always at pains to express his own emotional response to reality, whether that reality was the general suffering of mankind, the women in his life, or the everyday objects that surrounded him – his pets, his pipe and tobacco, the glasses, books, masks, tapestries and accumulated paraphernalia of his studio. It was his personal response to these things that mattered. 'I find it monstrous,' he would say, 'that a woman should paint a pipe, because she doesn't smoke it.' He wanted his own paintings to 'give off emotion'.

'Reality' in art for Picasso did not necessarily mean a literal transcription of what he saw in front of him. He wanted to express the essence of the subject, and if that meant 'abstracting' or taking away unnecessary elements, or transforming the subject, then he would follow that course. He never thought in terms of concrete or abstract forms, only of what those forms meant to him.

Sometimes Picasso painted in a more

The Three Dancers (1925)
(right) Picasso began work on this monumental painting at a time when his marriage to Olga was becoming an increasing source of unhappiness and frustration. His bitterness is expressed in the frenzied spirit of the dance – a savage parody of the grace and classical beauty of ballet. The life-size figures are aggressively distorted in a wild celebration of Picasso's own creative and destructive energies.

The She-Goat (1950)
(left) Picasso constructed the plaster original of this sculpture – here in bronze – from a wicker basket (for the pregnant belly), palm leaves (for the ribs and backbone), scraps of iron (for the bony shoulders) and ceramic pots (for the udders).

Musée Picasso, Paris

naturalistic manner, as during the Blue and Rose periods, and sometimes in a less naturalistic one – his Cubist paintings for example. He believed all manners were equally valid, but he never adhered to the academic principles of beauty, and he soon broke away from his youthful training in the academic tradition: 'Art is not the application of a canon of beauty, but what the instinct and the brain can conceive beyond any canon. When we love a woman we don't start measuring her limbs. We love with our desires . . .'

The only comment on art Picasso ever wrote down himself (as opposed to the opinions that were recorded in interviews or by his friends) was, 'Painting is stronger than I am. It makes me do what it wishes.' This illustrates his approach very well. Painting, Picasso found, was an unloading of visions and sensations, and it was the creative process itself that was important. Watching him draw, one might have seen a bunch of flowers undergo several transformations, becoming a fish, then a cock and finally the head of a faun. Picasso took canvases through many stages like this, always trying to capture the spontaneous or impulsive idea, without finishing or killing it off.

Picasso could work with or without a model. After 80 sittings with Gertrude Stein, for example, he found he was still dissatisfied with her 'naturalistic' portrait. Rubbing the head out with turps, Picasso returned to the canvas much later and finished off the portrait in one session without her. Alternatively, he often used a model for the most 'abstract' of his Cubist portraits.

The Vollard Suite: no. 38 (1933)
(below) Picasso's 100 etched drawings, which were published by the great art dealer, Ambroise Vollard, explore the beauty and simplicity of pure line.

Primitive Sculpture

In the early years of the 20th century, several of Picasso's artistic contemporaries began to collect the African masks and strange primitive sculptures that they found gathering dust in Parisian bars. Picasso bought pieces from a dealer in the Rue de Rennes and, from 1907, when he painted *Les Demoiselles d'Avignon*, he started to use totem figures and masks in his paintings. His imagination was excited by the barbaric power of these sculptures, with their disregard for the classical canons of beauty, and by their abstract delight in form.

P. A. Ferrazzini

Barbier-Mueller Collection, Geneva

Babangi Mask, French Congo
(above) Avant-garde artists, including Matisse and Picasso, recognized the raw vitality and emotional force of African art.

AISA

Archaeological Museum, Barcelona

Iberian votive sculpture
(left) Picasso was fascinated by the stylizations of Iberian sculpture and he bought two examples from a friend who had stolen them from the Louvre.

With or without a model, Picasso never strayed 'out of reality', although he was claimed by the Surrealists as an influence, and because of his Cubism, was seen as the forefather of the abstract painters. Even when breaking up a subject into geometrical Cubist forms, releasing painting from the need to imitate natural forms, Picasso always used a subject: a figure, a landscape, or a collection of still-life objects. 'A few strokes of a brush that have no meaning will never make a picture', he once said. 'My brushstrokes always signify something – a bull, an arena, the sea, the mountains, the crowd . . . to arrive at abstraction it is always necessary to begin with a concrete reality. . . . Art is a language of symbols. Two holes – that's the symbol for the face, enough to evoke it without representing it. But isn't it strange that it can be done through such simple means?'

Picasso also made some extraordinary innovations in the field of sculpture. In 1912, he produced *Guitar*, the first sculpture not to be made by carving or modelling, but by 'assembling' different objects and materials in a revolutionary new departure. It was at this period that he was exploring new forms of Cubist painting, making collages with various shapes of different materials stuck onto the canvas – the first paintings with no oil paint. And he was also making three-dimensional assemblies on canvas, objects which are neither paintings nor sculptures.

In the late 1920s, Picasso started to make open wire constructions that looked like 'drawing in space'. Always eager to learn new techniques, he took a friend Julio Gonzalez to Boisgeloup and learned about metalwork construction from him. These new 'sculptures' had no centre and no mass, but although the formal abstract qualities were very important, Picasso was never interested in purely abstract sculpture. He often returned to more conventional sculptures of the human face and figure if he felt he was straying too far.

FEMALE INSPIRATION

The human figure remained Picasso's greatest and most lasting inspiration throughout all the periods: Blue, Rose, 'Negro' (when he was admiring the simple shapes and expressive power of primitive Negro and Polynesian statues), Cubist and Classical alike. It was most often the female figure, inspired by the different women in his own life. Sometimes these women were subject to grotesque deformations in Picasso's art, usually when his own emotional life was in turmoil. In these works, he was again expressing his own emotional and erotic response, which he believed was more truthful than any conventional likeness.

Picasso had strange working methods. Whenever he could, he liked to work at night, and preferred artificial light which he found more constant and 'exciting'. Colour in fact was less important to him than line, form and composition, and that is probably why he often worked in monochrome, or near-monochrome, as during the Blue, Rose and Cubist periods. Although he knew Matisse, and had a great respect for him, Picasso was not particularly interested in Matisse's decorative and abstract use of intense colour.

Picasso's whole life was spent pursuing new discoveries. He had an incredible visual memory, and from the start was able to grasp different techniques and assimilate the elements of different styles, always making them into something personal. But he was never satisfied with one discovery – it urged him on to the next. As an old man he took up ceramics at the Madoura potteries in Vallauris, and discovered new techniques and glazes, and ways of giving texture and pattern to the surface by impressing objects like leaves. Similarly, he turned linocutting into a more versatile and expressive medium.

'The essential thing in our period of weak morale is to create enthusiasm', Picasso remarked to a friend. 'Enthusiasm is what we need most, we and the younger generation.' Because of his inexhaustible creativity and variety, Picasso has been claimed by many 20th-century artistic movements as their innovator and inspiration.

LOOKING AT A MASTERPIECE

Seated Woman (Marie-Thérèse Walter)

In January 1937, Picasso painted a series of portraits of his young mistress, Marie-Thérèse. The two had become lovers some ten years earlier and the liaison had brought Picasso's life a new happiness and calm. In this smiling portrait, Marie-Thérèse's harmonious form has been deliberately distorted, to incorporate several views in one image. Picasso did not necessarily set out with this intention. He has concentrated on Marie-Thérèse's most salient features – her drowsy eyes, relaxed hands, rounded form and her patterned dress and hat: but, in the process of painting, the sitter has undergone a transformation, as Picasso has become immersed in the curving rhythms of his subject overall. In essence, however, Picasso's emotional response to Marie-Thérèse's qualities – her serene, contemplative nature and voluptuous sensuality – has produced, at least, just as true and beautiful a portrait as any conventional likeness.

'Why should I try to imitate nature?
I might just as well try
to trace the perfect circle.'

Picasso

Visual Arts Library/©DACS 1987

Musée Picasso, Paris

© DACS 1987

TRADEMARKS

Distortion

Picasso often subjects his forms to grotesque distortions, allowing his initial idea the same mobility as his thoughts. He once stated: 'I paint what I know, not what I see' – and, in a certain sense, when one *knows* that a face has two eyes, it can seem perverse to represent it with one. Picasso was aware that his distortions were often subversive but, as he explained, 'Whatever the source of the emotion that drives me to create, I want to give it a form which has some connection with the visible world, even if it is only to wage war on that world.'

Gallery

Picasso was so prolific and versatile that, for an understanding of his work, his career is usually divided into periods: the Blue period, of which the Girl in a Chemise is a typically melancholy example; the Rose period, with its cast of off-duty circus performers; and then the great breakthrough into Cubism, followed by the playful collages of Synthetic

© DACS 1987

Girl in a Chemise *c.1905*
28¾″ × 23¾″ Tate Gallery, London

The work of the Blue period is like painting in a minor key, to use a musical analogy. Picasso's figures are frail and wistful like those of the Pre-Raphaelite artist, Burne-Jones, who was one of his early enthusiasms. The figure has been deliberately flattened – a stylistic feature which points the way to Picasso's Cubist period.

Cubism. His works of the 1920s, such as Women Running on the Beach, show a Classical influence, while The Dream and similar works of the 1930s reveal a certain debt to Surrealism (as well as the all-embracing influence of Marie-Thérèse). Picasso himself said: 'I paint the way some people write their autobiography. The paintings, finished or not, are the pages of my journal, and as such, they are valid. The future will choose the pages it prefers. It's not up to me to make the choice.' Taken as a whole, Picasso's works are a radical assertion of the artist's right to create and not merely represent, and, above all, a triumphant affirmation of his love of life.

The Acrobat's Family with a Monkey *1905*
41″ × 29½″ Göteborgs Konstmuseum, Sweden

Picasso's Rose period is also sometimes known as his Circus period. He seems to have felt the same kind of fascination for circus performers as Degas for ballet dancers, and the same desire to show what they were like in real life, away from the limelight. As an artist, he found it easy to identify with these 'artistes' – they too were Bohemians and had special gifts, yet lived outside respectable society. This charming group of the acrobat with his wife and child recalls Italian Renaissance pictures of the Holy Family. The conjunction of this near-sacred image with that of the monkey may be a playful allusion to man's animal nature.

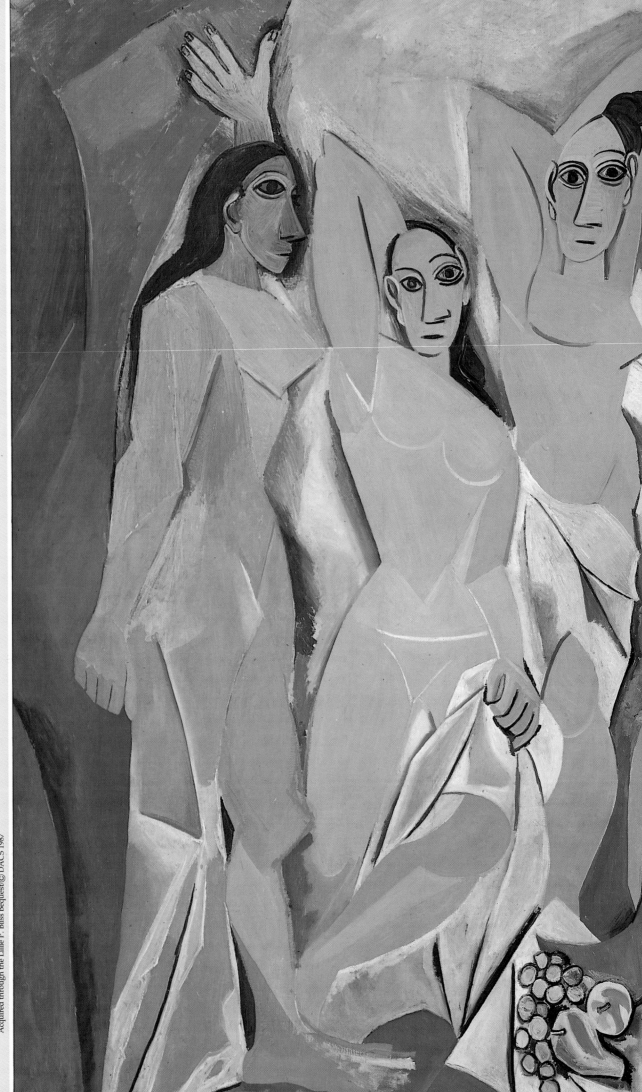

Les Demoiselles d'Avignon *(1907)*
96″ × 92″; oil on canvas
Collection, The Museum of Modern Art, New York

In this, the most wilfully and aggressively ugly of all his works, Picasso flouts two of the most obvious conventions by which a painter creates an illusion of reality: shading for mass and perspective for space. Where there is shading, it contradicts itself and refuses to convey any three-dimensional effect, and there is no use of traditional perspective. In addition, the figures have been fragmented and in this respect the work is the foundation-stone of Cubism. The painting is remarkable for combining utterly different styles within the same image: the three women to the left have faces modelled upon ancient Iberian sculptures, whereas the features of the other two come from African tribal masks. But the work does more than just attack an accepted style of painting. There is also a meaning. The women are prostitutes – the work takes its title from a street in the red-light district of Barcelona – and the fruit in the foreground is a fairly commonplace vanitas symbol, suggesting that all life, like a piece of ripe fruit, must eventually decay. Picasso originally intended to include the figures of a sailor and a medical student holding a skull, but probably decided that this would make his composition less arresting and his message a little too obvious.

57

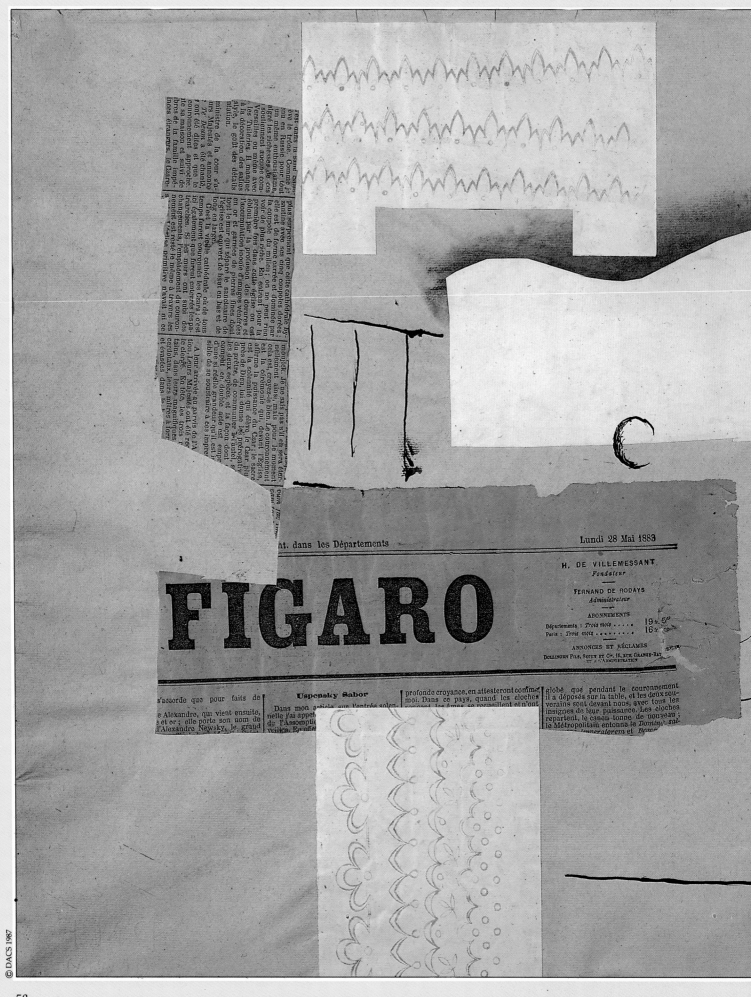

**Bottle of Vieux Marc, Guitar, Glass and
Newspaper** *1913*
18¼" × 24½" Tate Gallery, London

*This is a characteristic work of the Synthetic phase of
Cubism. It is more decorative and approachable than the
products of the earlier, straight-faced Analytical phase,
and it incorporates elements of collage. With typical
Cubist wit, the bottle is not represented in the round
but flattened out, a little like a cardboard cut-out that
can be folded and bent to form a three-dimensional
object. It is as if Picasso wished to point out that since a
picture is, after all, a flat object, why should it not show
things in a flat way? The newspaper is a joke at the
expense of naturalism: if painting is to imitate reality,
the painter might just as well stick real things on to the
canvas! This is brought into comic contrast with the
almost naïve stylization in the depiction of the guitar,
with the columns of print ingeniously made to mimic
the guitar's frets. Picasso's choice of newspaper is also
deliberate: Le Figaro is named after a character with
whom he could identify – the witty, energetic and
subversive Spanish hero of* The Marriage of Figaro
and The Barber of Seville.

Pablo Picasso

Women Running on the Beach 1922
13¼″ × 16¾″ Musée Picasso, Paris

Picasso's art developed by feeding off itself and sometimes by reacting against itself. We can only understand each individual work fully if we see how it relates to what came before, and the Women Running on the Beach is a case in point. If Cubism mocked the expectations of viewers who had been nourished on the values of traditional painting, then Picasso's Classical mode of the 1920s gave a jolt to those who had become used to his Cubist innovations. Colossal female figures thunder past, against a theatrical backdrop (an enlarged version of the design was later made as a ballet curtain), throwing their emphatically bulky limbs around with abandon. The attitude towards mass and space remains playful, but the means of subversion have changed from contradiction to virtual caricature. The sculptural look of the figures is mock-Classical; the draperies are vaguely Greco-Roman, and the poses are reminiscent of those reliefs that show ecstatically dancing Maenads, the female votaries of Bacchus. Picasso spent much of his time in the South of France from this time on, and the associations of the Mediterranean world inspired him to treat themes that were timeless and mythic in feeling.

Nude in a Red Armchair *1932*
51″ × 38¼″ Tate Gallery, London

The model for both the works shown here was the young Marie-Thérèse Walter, who became Picasso's mistress and later bore him a daughter, Maia. Their keynote is the curve; every form of Marie-Thérèse's body is soft, caressable and child-bearing. In the shape made by her hair there is even a hint of a Madonna's halo.

The Dream 1932
51¼″ × 38″ Mr and Mrs Victor W. Ganz, New York

*The most exciting new style in painting in the 1930s was Surrealism,
a celebration of the irrational workings of the unconscious mind.
Picasso took an interest in it, though from a distance, and the dream
is a favourite Surrealist theme. The face is a profile and full-face view
rolled into one, perhaps to suggest phases of the moon.*

AISA© DACS 1987

Guernica *1937*
137½″ × 305¾″ Casón del Buen Retiro, Madrid

Cubism forced the idea upon an unsuspecting world that forms in art need not be descriptive, and a work like Guernica *demonstrates how much more expressive they could be as a result. Violent things are happening, but it is the terrible jaggedness and criss-crossing of lines that create the mood of fear and confusion. The work was Picasso's reaction to a specific event, the bombing of the ancient Basque capital of Guernica by Franco's German allies in April 1937. But the result is a generalized image of man's inhumanity to man, part bullfight and part 'Massacre of the Innocents'.*

Reclining Nude with Necklace 1968
44¾″ × 63¾″ Tate Gallery, London

The distortion of form and the use of arbitrary colour can impart a greater degree of 'presence' to a figure than the most seamless naturalism. Here the nude seems to force herself upon our attention, the sense of raw physicality about her body heightened by the emphasis on the genitals, breasts and buttocks, and the gleeful disregard for anatomy that allows them all to be shown in the same view. Picasso's brushwork can denote joy, frenzy and even violence; it never stoops to prettiness. In the Reclining Nude with Necklace, *careless-looking scribbles and streaks of thicker paint are played off against thinner, flatter washes underneath. There is a delight here in the character of paint as a material, and in brushwork as the record of concentrated activity.*

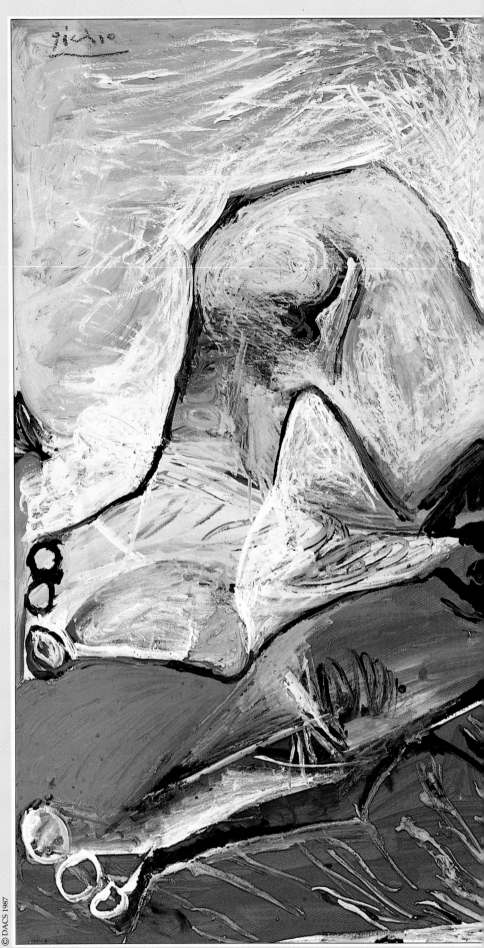

© DACS 1987

The Cubist Years

Abandoning the single, 'realistic' perspective of 19th-century art, Cubism introduced a variety of viewpoints to create a new and challenging relationship between the work and its spectator.

When Georges Braque first visited Picasso's Paris studio in September 1907, he was, like most observers, shocked by the ugliness and brutality of Picasso's *Les Demoiselles d'Avignon* (pp.56-7). Yet the experience of this revolutionary canvas was fundamental to Braque who, up until this point, had been painting successful canvases in the colourful Fauvist style. Despite his outrage, Braque realized that Picasso was hinting at a radical new approach to painting. Within eight months, Braque had followed up his experience in his giant *Standing Nude*, a dramatic figure composition which, even more than the *Demoiselles*, heralded the arrival of Cubism.

In 1909, Picasso and Braque embarked on a period of intense collaboration, working together to establish a new direction for the visual arts. Cubism was the product of this collaboration, which lasted until the outbreak of the First World War in 1914. By 1910, numerous, less talented artists were producing paintings in a Cubist style, and variations on the innovations of Picasso and Braque were being produced in great numbers until as late as 1925.

Picasso and Braque themselves did not see Cubism as a movement, or even a coherent style. The paintings which they produced during the pre-war years were largely painted to satisfy their own interests, and those of a few enlightened friends. 'During those years', Braque wrote, 'Picasso and I discussed things which nobody will ever discuss again, which nobody else would

Cézanne's guiding example
The late work of Cézanne – like this almost abstract landscape – was the dominant influence on Braque and Picasso in their Cubist period.

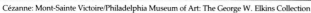
Cézanne: Mont-Sainte Victoire/Philadelphia Museum of Art: The George W. Elkins Collection

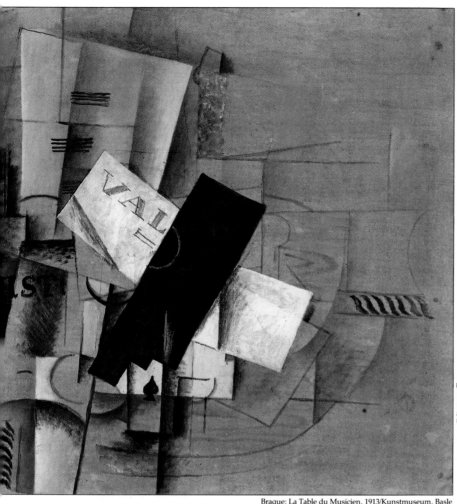

Braque: La Table du Musicien, 1913/Kunstmuseum, Basle

A voice for Cubism
Guillaume Apollinaire, here sitting in Picasso's studio, first introduced Braque to Picasso and acted as a spokesman for the Cubist movement as a whole.

Transforming reality
(left and above) On the wall of Braque's studio hang some of the objects – such as African masks and musical instruments – that he was to use as the basis for his still-lifes. But he never wanted to recreate these objects representationally. Instead, as The Musician's Table *of 1913 suggests, they are broken down into their basic shapes, so that the curves of a mandolin, the circles of a sound box and the flat edges of a fret board form patterns of contrast and harmony.*

know how to discuss, which nobody else would know how to understand.'

Because of the essentially private nature of their art, neither artist wrote a manifesto of Cubism, and their own views about their art are largely unknown. Two things, however, are clear. Firstly, Cubism was not intended to be an abstract art. However difficult they may be to decipher, true Cubist paintings were always intended to be representational, to reproduce an aspect of the real world. Secondly, both artists rejected the traditional assumption that a painting should represent the world exactly as it appears to us. They did not want to produce a mere likeness of the visual world, as a photographer might do. They wanted to represent the world in a less literal, more conceptual way.

CHALLENGING CONVENTION

The reality of an object or figure, they argued, does not stop at what we see of it at a single glance. It also comprises those views and aspects which we do not actually see at one glance but which, in our minds, we know to exist. An image which shows an object simultaneously from different points of view, while not strictly logical, may in fact be more realistic in that it presents a more complete picture of our experience and knowledge of the object. 'There is no certainty except in what the mind conceives', Braque wrote.

Inevitably, Picasso and Braque abandoned traditional methods of representation. They moved away from conventional perspective, which constructs for the viewer a 'realistic' space, as seen from one point of view. Instead of this, they placed their objects in a space which, while it may be convincing, is ambiguous and difficult to read. They abandoned the realistic use of light and shade, introducing a more complex system which often serves to flatten objects, rather than to create a convincing illusion of relief. Most important, they broke up the objects and figures in their paintings, presenting them as a series of geometric facets, which combine into simultaneous views.

During the early years of Cubism, both painters were influenced by the late works of Cézanne. Cézanne's influence on Braque was particularly marked. In the summer of 1908, Braque produced a series of still-lifes and landscapes which clearly reflect his technique of reducing forms to bold, geometric shapes. Following Cézanne, Braque learned to merge together the planes of foreground and background to create a shifting, ambiguous space – a technique which he developed further during the years of Analytical Cubism. On his return to Paris, Braque showed these landscapes in the 1908 Salon. Reviewing the

The third Cubist
Although he did not begin painting seriously until 1911, Juan Gris was the only contemporary of Braque and Picasso to be accepted as a true Cubist. Bold in his use of colour and highly geometrical in his approach to form, Gris took Cubism to its most advanced stages. In this painting of 1913, it is the landscape of Céret – a town in southern France frequented by Braque and Picasso – which is transformed through Gris' kaleidoscopic harmonies.

Gris: Paysage à Céret, 1913/Moderna Museet, Stockholm

Salon, the critic Louis Vauxcelles remarked that Braque 'reduced everything to cubes'. From this point onwards, Braque, Picasso and his followers were generally referred to as Cubists, although it was not a label the artists themselves used.

Between 1909 and 1912, Picasso and Braque created the first distinctive phase of Cubism, known as Analytical Cubism. During this period the artists dissected, or 'analysed', the objects they painted, attempting to find a set of forms which could suggest the reality of the whole. They then 'reconstructed' the object in patterns of overlapping shapes painted in monochrome, and set in an indeterminate space. The 'recognizable' parts of each object were scattered throughout the picture – a fragment of lettering, a bottle, a violin – merged with other, more ambiguous forms or put together in surprising combinations.

THE NEW COLLAGES

In 1912, Braque and Picasso, realizing perhaps that Analytical Cubism was becoming more and more abstract, adopted a different approach, now known as Synthetic Cubism. The most important aspect of this development was the introduction of collage. Instead of breaking down their objects into facets and 'reconstructing' them, Braque and Picasso started with a set of ready-made fragments or 'certainties' – wallpaper, fake chair caning, newspaper and patches of paint – which they built up, or synthesized, into more concrete images.

The technique of collage also allowed the artists to indicate spatial relationships more clearly without resorting to the use of conventional perspective. A glass drawn on top of a piece of pasted newspaper could be understood as a glass

Roger Viollet

The end of an era
(above) As a movement, Cubism collapsed with the outbreak of the First World War. Braque, Léger and Apollinaire went away to fight. Left alone, Picasso changed style and direction and only Gris, in poverty and loneliness, continued to paint Cubist pictures, developing the Cubist idiom into his own personal language.

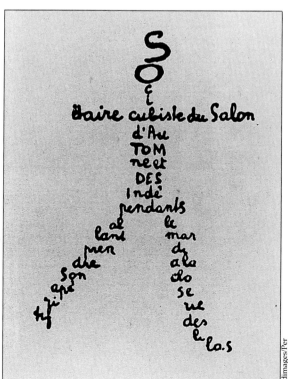

Edimages/Per

Word-pictures
(left) In the same way that Braque and Picasso introduced materials like rope and newspaper print into their paintings, so Apollinaire began to explore the visual possibilities of poetry. His calligrammes, *or word-pictures, are efforts to free language from the restrained academicism of contemporary poetry. This whimsical example translates simply as: 'Cubist member of the Autumn and Independent Salon on his way to drink his aperitif on a Tuesday at the Closerie des Lilas.'*

actually standing on a newspaper, without recourse to a 'realistic' perspective. At the same time, by using the materials of everyday life, the artist could further challenge traditional assumptions about the nature and purpose of art. The artist did not have to reproduce the textures of objects illusionistically, through the skilful use of brush – he could introduce them directly, by using the materials themselves.

That is not to say that Picasso and Braque always used collage realistically. They clearly delighted in using familiar materials in unfamiliar ways – turning a piece of newspaper into a violin, for example, or a piece of wallpaper into a table-top. In so doing, they challenged the notions of reality and of illusion in ever more complex and sophisticated ways.

It was also during 1912 that Picasso made his first Cubist sculpture, transforming the principles of his collages into three dimensions. His revolutionary 'constructions' were made from a variety of materials, including wire and sheet-metal. As with the collages, the radical element in Picasso's sculptures lay partly in his introduction into the medium of ordinary objects and substances, not normally associated with fine art.

Despite their numerous followers, Picasso and Braque accepted only one other artist as a true Cubist – the painter Juan Gris who, from 1911 onwards, was painting 'analytical' works in a highly geometric style, with bold accents of colour. Gris also produced some of the most sophisticated and decorative of the Cubist paper collages or *papier-collés*. Apart from Gris, few of the followers of Braque and Picasso remained faithful to the principles of pure Cubism. While artists such as Delaunay and Léger adopted Cubist forms and structures in their paintings, their works moved increasingly away from the representation of objects, towards the inevitable development of a purely abstract art.

A Year in the Life 1937

Picasso's famous *Guernica* is the artist's outraged response to an atrocity committed during the Spanish Civil war. Here, as elsewhere in Europe, Fascism was on the march. At this time, France was dangerously divided, Russia was in turmoil, and Britain was initiating a policy of appeasement with Germany.

On 26 April 1937, the small undefended Basque town of Guernica was bombed for three hours, killing and wounding 2,000 civilians. This atrocity was the work of the élite German Condor Legion, sent to Spain by Adolf Hitler. Both Nazi Germany and Fascist Italy were aiding General Franco and his Nationalist rebel army against the elected Spanish government, partly through ideological sympathy and partly in order to gain operational experience in preparation for more serious conflicts. In 1937, however, the wanton destruction of civilians was new enough to be considered shocking and both the Nationalists and the Nazis disclaimed responsibility, falsely asserting that the retreating Basques were responsible.

Britain and France's decision not to intervene on the Republican side gave the Nationalists, supported by Italy and

JEAN GABIN
PIERRE FRESNAY
et
ERIC VON STROHEIM
dans

LA GRANDE ILLUSION

Adaptation et dialogues de
JEAN RENOIR et **CHARLES SPAAK**

Musique de **KOSMA**

Un film de
JEAN RENOIR

avec **DALIO**

The Great Illusion (1937)
(left) This powerful anti-war film was directed by Jean Renoir, son of the painter Pierre-Auguste Renoir. His experiences of the First World War and increasing fears that Europe would once again become a battleground prompted Renoir to make a film that would persuade people of the illusory nature of the barriers between nations, whether racial, political, economic or physical. The film was awarded a special prize at the Venice Film Festival the same year, only to be banned in Fascist Italy and Nazi Germany.

Germany, an overwhelming advantage leaving only the Soviet Union to assist the beleaguered Spanish Republic with supplies. But, when 'unknown' (actually Italian) submarines sank British and French merchant ships trading with the Republic, the two powers called a conference at Nyon and anti-submarine patrols were set up to stop the sinkings.

Despite this example of firmness, Britain became committed to a policy of appeasement in 1937. Stanley Baldwin retired with an earldom and Neville Chamberlain became Prime Minister. Chamberlain believed that, since the League of Nations had failed to stop Italian and German aggression in Abyssinia and the Rhineland, the only rational course was to negotiate with the two powers and meet their more urgent demands. The Dominions agreed with Chamberlain at the Imperial Conference of 1937. In November, Lord Halifax was sent to see Hitler to discuss the Sudeten German minority in Czechoslovakia which, encouraged by the Nazis, had already become restive. This policy was to lead in 1938 to the Munich agreement and the dismemberment of Czechoslovakia.

FASCISM ADVANCES UNCHECKED

Other European powers who might have opposed Fascism were in disarray. In France, Leon Blum's Popular Front government of Radicals, Socialists and Communists resigned in June 1937. The situation was even worse in the Soviet Union, where the Stalinist purges of the Old Bolsheviks had entered a third year. Karl Radek and other prominent Party members

Shanghai under fire
(right) Japanese hunger for empire had led to the invasion of Manchuria in 1931. But full-scale war against China did not erupt until after a clash of opposing forces near Peking in July 1937. By the end of the year, Peking, Shanghai and Nanking had fallen to the invader.

'Degenerate' art
(above) This photograph records Hitler's official visit in June 1937 to the Nazi-organized Exhibition of Degenerate Art which attempted to ridicule the work of modern masters such as Kirchner, Picasso and Klee. Independent thought and creativity were intolerable to a régime determined to control both art and culture.

Golden Gate Bridge
(left) The Golden Gate is a three mile stretch of water between the two promontories of San Francisco in the south and Marin County in the north, enclosing San Francisco Bay. On 27 May 1937, the two areas were officially joined by a suspension bridge after four years work at a cost of 35 million dollars.

were tried as 'Trotskyites' and a few months later the distinguished Marshal Tukashevsky and seven of his colleagues were court martialled. All were executed. A semblance of normality was restored only after new show trials in March 1938 which eliminated the last possible rivals to Stalin.

In the Far East, the Japanese launched a full-scale invasion of China, relentlessly bombing target cities. Peking and Shanghai fell and by December 1937 they had captured Nanking, where a blood bath was perpetrated that cost tens of thousands of Chinese lives. Nevertheless, resistance remained unbroken and the war which tied down a million Japanese soldiers soon became a liability, creating many of the problems that eventually caused Japan to plunge into the Second World War.

There were many other events in 1937. The British Parliament reformed the divorce laws; for the first time, desertion and insanity became grounds for divorce, and the waiting period was reduced from six months to six weeks. Britain's ex-King, Edward VIII, now the Duke of Windsor, married Mrs Simpson, the woman for whom he had renounced his throne the year before. The skull of Pithecanthropus, an extinct form of man, was discovered in Java; despite his receding forehead and lack of chin, he was an intelligent being, since later evidence showed that he had learned to use fire. The American chemist, Wallace H. Carothers, was granted a posthumous patent on a synthetic material named nylon, which his employers, Du Pont, proceeded to use for the manufacture of ladies' stockings. And the world's first turbo jet engine was tested on 12 April 1937 by Frank Whittle.

Archiv für kunst und Geschichte

Great American writer

(above) Ernest Hemingway published his novel To Have and Have Not in October 1937. The story centres around the luckless Harry Morgan, boat-owner turned smuggler, who is a typical Hemingway hero in his stoical fortitude in the face of intolerable odds. In the same year, Hemingway returned to Spain, now racked with civil war, as a journalist and chairman of the Ambulance Committee for the American Friends of Spanish Democracy.

Call for volunteer aid

(right) This poster of 1937 pleads for support of the Republican cause in the Spanish Civil War in the face of official French and English neutrality. Many thousands of adventurous young men, including writers such as George Orwell, W. H. Auden and Ernest Hemingway, volunteered to serve in the International Brigades organized from Paris by the Russians, while a lesser number fought on the Nationalist side.

Jean-Loup Charmet

UMBERTO BOCCIONI

1882-1916

Umberto Boccioni was the most gifted artist of the Italian Futurist movement, and one of its most intelligent spokesmen. Born in southern Italy in 1882, he moved to Rome aged about 18 and began his career in the studio of a commercial artist. In Rome, his contact with the Italian avant-garde helped develop his interest in modern city life as a subject for his painting, and stimulated his taste for industrial themes.

Boccioni's art did not mature, however, until around 1910, after he had come into contact with Marinetti, the leader of the Futurist movement which had taken Europe by storm at the beginning of the previous year. Thereafter, Boccioni's short career was closely tied to the development of Futurism, which lasted until the outbreak of war. In 1916, after a year of active service, he died in a riding accident. He was just 33.

Arrogance and Excess

**Energetic, persuasive and ruthlessly ambitious, Boccioni
wholeheartedly embraced the Futurist goals. But his early brilliance
was extinguished by a fatal riding accident.**

Boccioni: Controluce; La Madre/Lovisatti Collection, Treviso

Cecilia, was the main emotional focus of his life –
Boccioni never married – and was also a staunch
supporter of his art. In the war diary which he kept
in 1915, Boccioni relates how his mother followed
him and his fellow volunteers (members of the
Lombard Volunteer Cyclist Battalion) in a carriage
shouting, 'Long live the Futurists, Long live Italy,
Long live the volunteers!'

In 1898 or 1899, Boccioni left home and moved to
Rome to continue his artistic studies. Significantly,
he did not follow a formal academic training but,
on his father's instructions, entered the studio of a
commercial artist. The rejection of traditional art
and culture was to become one of the great rallying
cries of the Futurist movement, and Boccioni's
unconventional beginnings probably helped foster
his sympathy with this position. Nonetheless,
while Boccioni opposed the systematic study of
classical models (which formed the basis of a
formal training), he displayed a keen interest in the
art of the past. The drawings of his Roman period
include copies of antique statues, and of works by
the Renaissance Old Masters, as well as cityscapes,
modern street scenes and studies of cars – all of
which were to become favourite Futurist themes.

The decisive event of Boccioni's Roman years
was his encounter, in 1901, with the artist Giacomo

Umberto Boccioni was born in Reggio Calabria, on
the southern tip of Italy, on 19 October 1882. His
father was a government official whose job
involved extensive travel within Italy, and during
Boccioni's early years the family lived in places as
far afield as Genoa, Padua and Forlì.

In 1897, Boccioni went with his family to Sicily,
where he completed his basic education at the
Technical Institute of Catania, displaying an early
interest in literature and drawing. He was not,
however, a precocious draughtsman, and only
gained average marks for his drawing studies.

Little is known of Boccioni's relationship with
his father, Raffaele, who does not seem to have
favoured his son's artistic ambitions. Throughout
his life, however, Boccioni remained close to his
mother and to his sister Amelia, both of whom
appear frequently in his works. His mother,

A devoted mother
*(above) Cecilia Boccioni
was a dominant influence
on her son's life. She
actively supported his
artistic ambitions and
posed endlessly for
drawings, paintings and
sculptures.*

The artist's birthplace
*(right) Boccioni was born
in Reggio Calabria. The
city's classical remains
would have made little
impression on the artist,
who displayed a preference
for industrial cityscapes.*

A commercial artist
(right) After training in a commercial studio in Rome, Boccioni was forced to earn his living by producing illustrations. This design, for the Italian Automobile Club, heralds his preoccupation with cars and speed.

Key Dates

1882 born in Reggio Calabria, Italy

1898/99 moves to Rome

1901 meets Balla and works in his studio

1906 visits Paris and travels to Russia

1907 settles in Milan

1910 co-writes the *Manifesto of Futurist Painters*

1910-11 paints *The City Rises*

1911 returns to Paris to study Cubism

1912 Futurist exhibition held in Paris

1915 volunteers for war service

1916 killed in a riding accident

Automobile e caccia alla volpe/Automobile Club d'Italia

Balla, whose studio at the Porta Pinciana provided a meeting place for Rome's artistic and literary avant-garde. Balla was a master of the Divisionist style, a technique of painting in dots of pure colour, derived from the French Neo-Impressionists. Unlike many contemporary artists, Balla also had an interest in low-life themes – themes of work and city life, which reflected the reality of the technological age.

Balla's style and subject-matter appealed to Boccioni. He studied with Balla for several months, and probably frequented his studio throughout his time in Rome. Also studying with Balla was the painter Gino Severini, who later joined the Futurists. He and Boccioni became close friends, sharing an interest in the writings of Nietzsche, Marx and Engels.

cafés, the brightly painted women and the 'bizzare' dancing at the Moulin de la Galette, where he gained free admission in order to draw.

These violent moods were typical of Boccioni, who was a complex and difficult character. Although frequently racked by self-doubt, Boccioni was egocentric, aggressive and ruthlessly ambitious – Severini caustically described him as 'Napoleon come back to life'. He was frequently jealous of the success of others and prone to fits of depression when he was not at the forefront of the

Inspiring company
(below) During his years in Rome, Boccioni studied with Giacomo Balla – shown here with his family. Balla immediately won Boccioni's admiration and respect.

Grazia Neri, Milan

FINDING AN IDENTITY

Boccioni stayed in Rome until March 1906, and made periodic trips to Padua to see his mother and sister. But despite his artistic contacts and a relatively stimulating environment, Boccioni was restless and unhappy. Although he was influenced by Balla and admired his work, he had difficulty establishing a clear direction for his own art. He was also plagued by financial worries and was forced to make his living by commercial designing, producing illustrations for Italian magazines. Shortly after his departure for Paris at the end of March, he wrote bitterly to his family of the hardships of his Roman years, declaring that 'in Rome I got to such a point that I thought I would have to shoot myself . . . I haven't studied for two years because of those wretched designs. They ruined my nerves, I have been contaminated by that infernal business, and who knows if I shall ever recover.'

At the same time, Boccioni was intoxicated by the experience of Paris and wrote excitedly of the trams, the subways with their electric lights, the

Workshops at Porta Romana/Banca Italiana Commerciale, Milan

A Futurist theme
(left) In 1907, Boccioni moved to Porta Romana, Milan, to live with his mother and sister. Pastels and paintings of the time show his fascination with the surrounding industrial landscape.

Leading lights
(below) Following an enthusiastic reception in Milan, the Futurist exhibition travelled to Paris, accompanied by Boccioni and Marinetti (on the right) – the founding father of the Futurist Movement.

action. Significantly, Boccioni's days of active war service seem to have been the happiest of his life, and it seems likely that much of the attraction of Futurism for Boccioni lay in its theatrical and self-advertising character.

Boccioni stayed in Paris until July 1906, when he made a brief trip to Russia. At the end of the year he returned to Italy, and in 1907 he moved to Milan, settling with his mother and sister in the industrial suburb of Porta Romana. He was to remain based in Milan until 1915.

By 1907, Boccioni had clearly identified what it was he wanted to achieve in his art, declaring 'I feel that I want to paint the new, the fruit of our industrial age.' But he remained uncertain about the form that his vision should take and had, as yet, produced no major works.

THE BEGINNINGS OF FUTURISM

In 1909, however, an event took place which was to change the course of Boccioni's life. On 20 February, Filippo Tommaso Marinetti, an Italian poet, launched *The Founding and Manifesto of Futurism*, published on the front page of the prestigious French newspaper *Le Figaro*. The publication caused a sensation and set the tone for the successive development of the Futurist movement, declaring: 'We intend to sing the love of danger, the habit of energy and fearlessness. Courage, audacity and revolt will be the essential elements of our poetry. We affirm that the world's magnificence has been enriched by a new beauty, the beauty of speed . . . We will glorify war . . . destroy the museums, libraries and academies of every kind.'

Marinetti was an outrageous and flamboyant figure, a superb organizer and a brilliant publicist. In 1910, he was subjected to three obscenity trials following the publication of his novel *Mafarka Futurista*, whose Futurist hero swaggers through life endowed with an 11-metre long penis, which he wraps around himself while he sleeps.

Marinetti turned the publicity continually to his own advantage and frequently resurrected the affair at his famous Futurist Evenings in order to provoke the audience.

The Futurist Manifesto was a virulent attack on established culture, but it was not primarily concerned with the visual arts. Shortly after its publication however, Marinetti met and joined forces with Boccioni, and with the painters Luigi Russolo and Carlo Carrà, and began to consider the role of painting within the Movement. One night early in 1910, the four men got together in Marinetti's house in Milan to draft the *Manifesto of Futurist Painters*, which was written the following morning in a milk bar near Porta Vittoria. The Manifesto was published as a leaflet by Marinetti's magazine *Poesia* on 11 February 1910, and was publicly declaimed by Boccioni from the stage of Turin's Chiarella Theatre in March. Balla and Severini also put their names to the document.

From this point onwards, Boccioni's life was inextricably linked with the development of the Futurist movement. Together with the other Futurists, who included poets and musicians, he set up exhibitions, issued countless manifestos and participated in Futurist Evenings held in theatres throughout the country.

The *Manifesto of Futurist Painters* enabled Boccioni to set out in concrete form many of his preoccupations of the previous ten years. The Manifesto stated: 'We are sickened by the foul laziness of artists who have endlessly exploited the glories of the ancient Romans . . . We must breathe in the tangible miracles of contemporary life – the iron network of speedy communications which envelops the earth, the transatlantic liners, those marvellous flights which furrow our skies . . . How can we remain insensible to the frenetic life of our great cities.' By the end of 1910, Boccioni had produced his first identifiably Futurist

Futurist Sculpture

Boccioni began working in sculpture around 1912. It was a medium which immediately fired his imagination, and in March 1912, he wrote, 'I am obsessed these days by sculpture. I think I can perceive a complete revival of this mummified art.' Most of Boccioni's sculpture has been destroyed, but from the pieces which remain it is clear that sculpture was the medium best suited to express his idea that even static forms extend or 'continue' into the space around them. In sculpture, he could show the dynamic extension of forms in three dimensions, a problem which he never really resolved in his painting. This theory of 'absolute motion' is most clearly expressed in his sculpture of a bottle (p.83). In his figure sculpture, Boccioni combined this idea with a more straightforward representation of movement forward through space, culminating in the explosive, and still remarkably 'modern', *Unique Forms of Continuity in Space (1913)*.

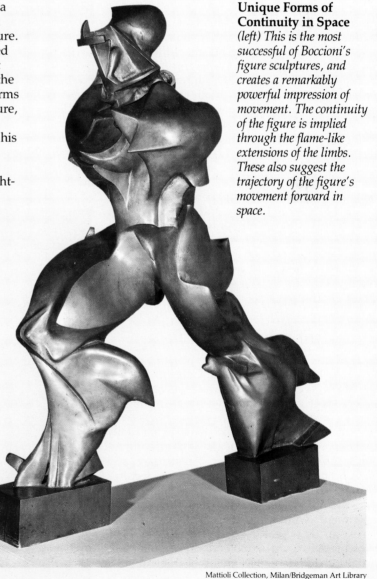

Unique Forms of Continuity in Space
(left) This is the most successful of Boccioni's figure sculptures, and creates a remarkably powerful impression of movement. The continuity of the figure is implied through the flame-like extensions of the limbs. These also suggest the trajectory of the figure's movement forward in space.

Synthesis of Human Dynamism (1913)
(left) This plaster sculpture (now destroyed), was probably the first of Boccioni's striding figures, and lacks the freedom of movement achieved in the later versions. The square shape around the head is probably for structural support.

By 1913, Boccioni had begun to work and exhibit alone, more and more. His egotism and ambitiousness began to isolate him increasingly from his colleagues, and by 1914, he had begun to fall prey to fits of depression, aggravated by a growing sense of being overtaken in his art. In 1916, Boccioni wrote to a friend; 'The burden of having to elaborate in oneself a century of painting is terrible, so much more so when one sees the new arrivals to Futurism grasping the ideas, mounting them and galloping off at breakneck speed.'

On 15 September 1914, Boccioni and his friends burst into a gala evening of opera at Milan's Teatro del Verne, and ceremonially burnt an Austrian flag in condemnation of Italy's neutrality in the war which had recently broken out in Europe. They repeated the demonstration in the Milan Galleria the next day, and were subsequently arrested, although they were treated exceptionally well. Boccioni wrote to his mother; 'I am in a paying cell and lunch brought in from outside is excellent . . . Eating, drinking, sleeping and reading.'

In July 1915, with Italy now allied with Great Britain, France and Russia, Boccioni and a number of his Futurist friends volunteered for the war and were enrolled in the Lombard Volunteer Cyclist Battalion. These days of active service were some of the happiest of Boccioni's life. He wrote, 'I am camped face to face with the Germans, waiting from one day to the next. I am in excellent health, despite everything, and I am happy.'

Ironically, Boccioni died, not in the thick of battle, but on a routine military exercise. In 1916, he was assigned to an artillery regiment stationed outside Verona. On 16 August he fell from his horse and was fatally injured. He died the next day, just 33 years of age.

painting, *Riot in the Galleria* (p.91), and was at work on his masterpiece *The City Rises* (pp.92-3).

Futurism was a great popular success, and in April 1911 the first big exhibition of Futurist painting opened in Milan. By the middle of 1911 the painters were planning to launch themselves on Paris, still recognized as the centre of European art. Ironically, in view of their triumphant claims to modernity, the Milanese Futurists were still unaware of the revolutionary developments of Cubism which had been emerging in Paris since 1907. On his return to Milan that autumn, Severini, who remained based in Paris, was dismayed at their ignorance and urged them to visit the city. In November 1911, Boccioni and Carrà set off, at Marinetti's expense, to study the works of Picasso and Braque and, on their return, incorporated Cubist elements into their new works. Nonetheless, Futurism did not meet with unqualified approval in Paris, and came under fierce attack from the influential French critic Apollinaire, who dismissed Boccioni's ideas as 'sentimental and puerile'.

Eager volunteers
(above) This photograph, taken shortly after Boccioni enlisted with the Lombard Volunteer Cyclist Battalion, shows the artist and his Futurist friends in their new army uniforms. The architect Sant'Elia is on the left, Boccioni is in the centre, and Marinetti appears on the right. Of the three, only Marinetti survived the war.

THE PARIS EXHIBITION

The Futurist exhibition was shown in Paris in 1912, at the Bernheim-Jeune Gallery. Despite Apollinaire's criticisms, it was a considerable success, and gained extensive press coverage – Boccioni is said to have rushed up to passers-by in the street to show them his name in the daily newspapers. From Paris it travelled to London, Berlin, Brussels, The Hague, Amsterdam and Munich, accompanied by provocative lectures from the tireless Marinetti.

In the spring of 1912, Boccioni also began to experiment with sculpture, exhibiting several pieces at that year's Salon d'Automne. The following year, an exhibition of his sculpture inaugurated the establishment of a permanent gallery of Futurist art in Rome.

The Glorification of War

From their earliest days the Futurists had glorified war, described by Marinetti as the 'Sole Hygiene of the World'. For Boccioni, who was by nature both restless and aggressive, war seemed particularly appealing, offering him a means of positive action and a way of escaping from the doubts and conflicts posed by his art. He was clearly exhilarated by the threat of constant danger, and wrote excited letters home from the Front, describing the progress of the fighting in graphic detail. In 1915, after an action which resulted in the Italians' capture of Dosso Casina, Boccioni wrote; 'War is a beautiful, wonderful, terrible thing. And in the mountains it seems like a battle with the infinite.' By 1916, however, when he returned to the Front, Boccioni had begun to be disillusioned with the reality of war and wrote; 'I shall leave this existence with a disdain for everything that is not art.'

Signora Busoni
(below) While he was on leave from the army in 1916, Boccioni stayed with the Busoni family at their villa outside Milan. During this peaceful interlude, he began to experiment with a new style inspired by Cézanne. This sunny portrait of his hostess tempts speculation as to how his art might have developed had he lived longer.

The Charge of the Lancers (1915)
(below) The theme of war was the perfect vehicle for Boccioni's interest in movement. Here, his characteristic lines of force become synonymous with the thrusting lines of the cavalry's lances. The figures are painted over a newspaper report of 4 January 1915, recording the taking of a strategic German position.

Boccioni's last moments
(right) Ironically, in view of his love of active service, Boccioni died, not in the thick of battle, but on a routine exercise with his cavalry regiment. On 16 August 1916, Boccioni fell while riding his horse around the outskirts of Verona. He died at dawn the following day. This photograph was taken shortly before the artist's untimely death.

Brera, Milan

Dynamic Visions

Boccioni's paintings and sculptures capture the exhilaration of movement, while also expressing the inner life of seemingly inanimate objects – the 'throbbing of their soul'.

In the *Technical Manifesto of Futurist Painters*, published in 1910, the Futurists boldly declared: 'The gesture which we would reproduce on canvas shall no longer be a fixed moment in universal dynamism. It shall simply be the dynamic sensation itself . . . all things move, all things run, all things are rapidly changing.' This preoccupation with movement was a constant feature of Futurism, but for Boccioni it assumed a special importance, and the depiction of the 'dynamic sensation' became the focus of his art.

Boccioni's interest in movement pre-dated the emergence of Futurism and can be traced back to the beginning of his career, in his early drawings of dancers, horses and motor cars. When, in 1909, Marinetti threw down the gauntlet, declaring that 'a roaring racing-car . . . is more beautiful than the Victory of Samothrace' (the famous classical statue), he was simply giving public expression to ideas that Boccioni had been formulating for the previous ten years.

While Futurism gave Boccioni a focus for his

The Street Enters the House (1911)
(right) In this garishly coloured work, Boccioni wanted the dominant sensation to be 'that which one would experience on opening a window: all life and the noises of the street rush in . . .'

Woman in a Garden (1910)
(below) Boccioni's early works anticipate the Futurist preoccupation with movement. Here, the vigorous strokes of pastel suggest the light swirling around the figures.

Giancarlo Costa

Banca Commerciale Italiana

ideas, it did not provide him with a solution to the technical problem of representing movement, and it was not until the end of 1910 that Boccioni began to find a way of formulating his vision.

In Boccioni's youth, Italian painting was a complex mixture of different trends. Boccioni later recalled that, at the time of his arrival in Rome, many young artists were turning for their inspiration to the Secessionist art of Klimt and the elegant forms of Art Nouveau. At the same time, much of Italian art was strongly Symbolist in feeling with an emphasis on emotional expression which particularly appealed to Boccioni. Boccioni was never simply interested in the physical aspect of movement. For him, it also had an emotional quality and he was, like the Symbolists, highly sensitive to the expressive potential of line. In an interview with Apollinaire, Boccioni described his

Umberto Boccioni

him to explore his interest in light effects, particularly in the garish quality imparted to objects by electric lighting, brilliantly captured in *Modern Idol* (p.96).

For Boccioni, however, no one had yet solved the problem of depicting movement as he saw it. Broadly speaking, movement, for Boccioni, had two aspects. Firstly, there was the movement of an object or figure from place to place, which is relative to our own position in space. Secondly, Boccioni argued, even objects which we think of as static, such as a bottle on a table, are in constant motion, both within themselves and in relation to the space around them. While we think that we see the world as a series of objects fixed in space, with clearly defined limits, we actually see a set of constantly shifting planes which mingle and interact. The painter must not simply capture one moment in the 'relative' motion of things – like a photographic 'still'. He must capture the actual sensation of universal flux.

Boccioni's first Futurist painting, *Riot in the Galleria* (p.91), only partly achieved this aim. Although the figures are in motion they seem 'frozen', and their forms are still clearly fixed in space. In 1911, however, Boccioni reached the first clear formulation of his ideas in *The Street Enters the*

Solidifying energy
(above) In sculpture, Boccioni arrogantly declared that he had found a way to revive this dead and 'static' art. His Development of a Bottle in Space *successfully captures the dynamism of his subject, as the energy at work within the bottle sets it spiralling into the surrounding space.*

Exhilarating speed
(below) This sketch for Dynamism of a Cyclist *is one of several works expressing 'that new absolute: velocity, which the truly modern temperament cannot disregard'.*

Niedersachische Landesgalerie, Hanover

paintings, illustrating *States of Mind* (p.95), saying: 'I have painted two canvases, one expressing departure, the other arrival . . . To mark the difference in feeling I have not used in my painting of arrival a single line from the painting of departure.'

Other artists, like Boccioni's friend and teacher Giacomo Balla, were experimenting with Signac's technique of Divisionism (a development of Pointillism), painting in small strokes of bright, unmixed colour, placed side by side on the canvas.

Boccioni was attracted by both these trends – Gaetano Previati, a painter who applied a Divisionist technique to Symbolist subject-matter of great emotional intensity, was an important influence on his early work. Boccioni discovered that Divisionism enabled him to give his canvases a vibrant, dynamic quality, while also allowing

Estorick Collection, London

The Laugh (1911)

(right) This work reveals Boccioni's fascination with the theories of the philosopher Henri Bergson: Bergson described the mechanism of laughter as 'a rationally structured system suddenly translated into a whirling machine'. What interested Bergson was the way laughter reverberated throughout the assembled company, encouraging participation in 'a kind of freemasonry or even complicity with other laughers'. Boccioni depicts the explosive effect of laughter by using expressionistic 'lines of force' and fragmented Cubist forms.

Images of gaiety

(below) The burst of laughter shatters the picture into a multitude of kaleidoscopic images, showing, as in this detail, people drinking, laughing and socializing under blazing artificial lights.

43⅜″ × 57¼″, oil on canvas

Collection, The Museum of Modern Art, New York. Gift of Herbert and Nannette Rothschild

House (pp.82-3). In this work, groups of overlapping planes represent objects without fixing them in space. The shifting configuration of shapes captures perfectly the 'dynamic sensation', and brilliantly conjures up the chaos and excitement of a busy modern street as it floods through the open window – the 'frenetic life' of the Futurists' Manifesto.

LINES OF FORCE

In *The City Rises* (p.92), Boccioni achieves a similar effect by different means, using 'lines of force'. These he defined as 'sheaves of lines corresponding to all the conflicting forces, following the general law of the violence of the picture'. As well as indicating directions of movement, these lines were designed to drag the spectator into the centre of the canvas 'so that he has to struggle with the figures in the picture'.

For Boccioni, the problem remained of how to show objects in a state of flux without dissolving them completely and making them unrecognizable. Apollinaire, the champion of Cubism, neatly identified this dilemma and shrewdly attacked the Futurists for their lack of 'plastic concern', their failure to capture the

substance of things.

In this respect the experience of Cubism was important for Boccioni, enabling him to bring greater solidity to his forms. The most successful product of the Cubist influence on Boccioni was the brilliant *States of Mind: The Farewells* (p.94), in which the Cubist shapes and lettering of the train combine with lyrical 'force-lines', which convey both the swirling motion of departure and the melancholy of the embracing figures.

Boccioni made his most successful studies of movement in sculpture, which partly solved the problem of creating solid forms. *The Development of a Bottle in Space* (p.83) is his clearest expression of the idea that apparently static forms extend into space, as the bottle 'uncurls' into the surrounding

atmosphere. In the exhilarating *Unique Forms of Continuity in Space* (p.79), Boccioni achieves a perfect synthesis of his two types of movement – the figure's striding movement forward through space and the 'absolute' movement of each part of the body, as it spirals out into the space around.

Most important of all, however, Boccioni's sculpture embodies Marinetti's idea of the Futurist superman, which he described in his tract *War, Sole Hygiene of the World*. This man will be 'built to withstand omnipresent speed. He will be endowed with unexpected organs adapted to the exigencies of continuous shocks . . . a prow-like development of the projection of the breast-bone which will increase in size as the future man becomes a better flyer.'

COMPARISONS
Poetry of Motion

The Futurists' preoccupation with movement was not unique. From 1911, Marcel Duchamp was experimenting with images of motion, inspired by chronophotography. His interest in movement seems to have arisen independently of the Futurists and, despite some similarities, his approach was fundamentally different. Duchamp was primarily interested in showing successive stages in one movement through space and, unlike Boccioni, was not concerned with the 'dynamic vibration' of the figure itself. In Boldini's work, movement is suggested by the furious, dashing application of paint.

Marcel Duchamp (1887-1968) **Nude descending a Staircase** *(below) Duchamp breaks up the figure's movement into its sucessive stages. The fragmented forms reveal the influence of Cubism on his work.*

Giovanni Boldini (1845-1931) **Pansies** *Boldini's paintings have been described as 'convulsive, whipped elegances', in which movement is suggested by electric flourishes of the brush.*

Emilia Boldini, Pistoia/Scala © DACS 1987

Philadelphia Museum of Art

The Louise and Walter Arensberg Collection © ADAGP 1987

The City Rises

The City Rises was Boccioni's first Futurist masterpiece, and was planned in the summer of 1910, shortly after the publication of the *Manifesto of Futurist Painters*. The subject of the painting is the awakening of a modern industrial city, which bursts into life as the people set about their work at the beginning of the day. Boccioni stated that his intention in the painting was 'to erect a new, vibrant and dynamic altar to modern life', while expressing the violence of the forces of progress.

The composition is dominated by the powerful form of a rearing horse, pulling its cart and rider along in its path. The horse is intended as a symbol of work, and is also a potent image of physical force. Its shape and movement recall the form of a wheel, and create a centrifugal force which drags the rest of the scene into action. The horse is set against the background of an industrial suburb, with unfinished buildings and smoking factory chimneys. Boccioni described the painting as 'a synthesis of work, light and colour'.

Mrs Simon Guggenheim Fund

Collection, The Museum of Modern Art, New York

Workers participation
(left) Boccioni's low viewpoint and whirlpool-like composition, pulls the spectator into the heart of the painting, inviting him to participate in the workers' struggle.

Love of horses
(above) Horses had always had a romantic appeal for Boccioni. This photograph shows him sketching a work-horse by the roadside during his first trip to Paris in 1906.

Private Collection

Estorick Collection, London

Boccioni: The City Rises (1910)

6'6½" × 9'10½", oil on canvas

Bridgeman Art Library

> 'No work which is not aggressive
> in character can be a masterpiece.'
> Marinetti

Beasts of labour
*(below) Work-horses were transformed by the Futurist
imagination into symbols of the industrial machine.*

Museum of Modern Art, New York/Winston Malbin Collection

Brera, Milan

Giancarlo Costa

Colour studies
(above) Boccioni made several powerful colour sketches for The City Rises, *in
which vibrant colours – fiery reds, blues, greens and yellows – create an
atmosphere of urgency and aggression, emphasized by the violent, flickering
brushwork and the dashing execution.*

Gallery

Although his career was tragically short and was interrupted by war service, Boccioni was a prolific artist. His energy comes out not only in the number of his works, but also in their dynamic character. Even in his early portraits, such as La Signora Massimino or Self-Portrait, there is vigour in the flickering brushwork, and in much of his

Signora Massimino *1908*
48½″ × 59½″ Private Collection

Boccioni produced many portraits, especially in the early part of his career. He had a penchant for painting elegant ladies in beautiful dresses and could doubtless have made a name for himself as a society portraitist. This picture is also known as 'The Woman at the Window', and the view through the glass shows a busy townscape of the type that was to inspire some of Boccioni's later work.

later work the expression of movement was his main concern. Until about 1911, Boccioni's paintings often show an interest in social themes, as in Riot in the Galleria and The City Rises, but thereafter he tended to use his pictures more as a vehicle for the expression of his theories on art than as commentaries on the life he saw around him. In works such as Dynamism of a Human Body, this led him to almost pure abstraction. In the final months of his life, Boccioni returned to naturalism in pictures such as his portrait of Ferruccio Busoni, but in a style very different from his early works, and there is no way of telling how he might have developed had he not died so young.

Self-Portrait *1908*
27½″ × 39½″ Brera, Milan

*As in the painting on the opposite page, Boccioni has given a large
area of the picture over to townscape, but the effect here is totally
different, the rather bleak buildings and streets serving to underline
the painter's tense expression. He holds a palette in his (unseen)
hand, but otherwise there is nothing to indicate that he is an artist,
and he seems concerned with some acute but unspecific cause.*

The Morning *1909*
23½″ × 21¾″ Private Collection

*This is one of the boldest of Boccioni's paintings of city life, both in the
powerful simplicity of the composition, based on the dominant
diagonal of the road, and in the intensity of the colouring, which
suggests the incipient heat of the day. In the background, smoke
billows from factory chimneys, underscoring the theme of labour.*

Giancarlo Costa

Riot in the Galleria *1910*
30″ × 25¼″ Brera, Milan

*This is the first of three pictures on the theme of confrontation
between police and demonstrators that Boccioni painted in 1910-11
and is one of the most brilliant expressions of his interest in
representing collective emotion. The scene is set in the Galleria
Vittorio Emanuele, an arcade that is one of the great sights of Milan.*

The City Rises (1910)
78½″ × 118½″; oil on canvas.
Collection, Museum of Modern Art, New York

This overpowering painting is one of Boccioni's most ambitious works, remarkable both for its sheer size and for the elaborate preparatory work he put into it. Boccioni was fascinated by the movement and bustle of modern city life, and in 1907 he wrote after a visit to Milan: 'I feel that I want to paint the new, the fruit of our industrial time. I am nauseated by old walls and old palaces, old motives, reminiscences . . . I want the new, the expressive, the formidable.' In The City Rises he brought together various impressions he had gained when making sketches in industrial parts of Milan and moulded them into a pulsating dynamic image dedicated to labour – when the picture was first exhibited it was entitled Lavoro (Work). *Dominating the picture are the huge work-horses that can be interpreted as representing the harnessed force of industry. In 1958, the painting was damaged in a fire at the museum, but it has been carefully restored.*

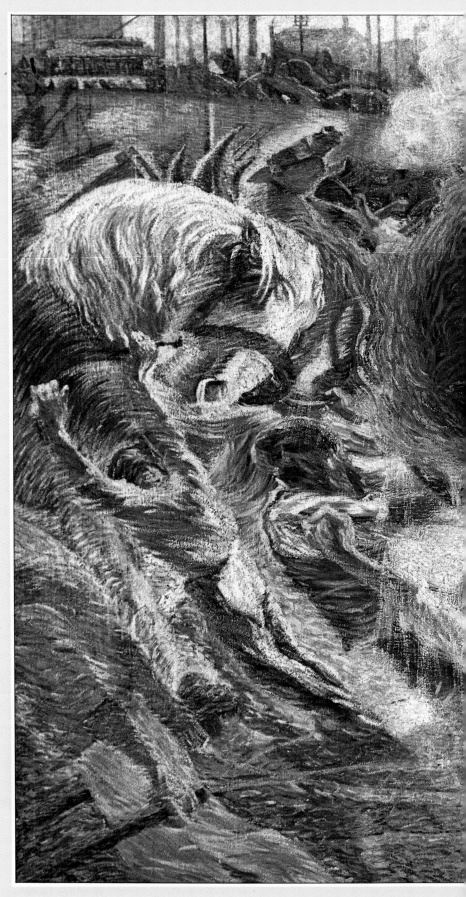

This and the painting opposite are part of a triptych (the third part is called
Those Who Stay) in which Boccioni depicted the various sights and
sensations experienced as a train pulls out of a station.

States of Mind: The Farewells (1911)
27³/₄″ × 37⅞″, oil on canvas. Collection, The Museum of Modern Art, New York

States of Mind: Those Who Go (1911)
27⅞" × 37¾"; oil on canvas. Collection, The Museum of Modern Art, New York

Here, the vividly coloured 'force-lines' are designed to express both the speed of the departing figures, and the excitement of leaving – the figures' own 'states of mind'.

95

Modern Idol *1911*
23½″ × 23″ Estorick Collection, London

*In the catalogue of an exhibition of Futurist paintings held at the
Sackville Gallery in London in 1912, this picture is described as
'Light effects upon the face of a woman' and it is the lurid lighting as
well as the woman's mesmeric stare that creates its unsettlingly
intense effect. It represents a Futurist version of the type of voracious
femme fatale so popular in painting at the turn of the century.*

Dynamism of a Human Body *1913*
39½″ × 39½″ Galleria d'Arte Moderna, Milan

Boccioni painted a series of works entitled 'Dynamism of . . .' (for instance, Dynamism of a Cyclist, Dynamism of a Footballer'), and in these his search for a pictorial means of representing the idea of speed led him almost to complete abstraction. Here, the fragmented but solid forms show the influence of the Cubist works of Picasso and Braque, which Boccioni had seen in Paris.

Dynamism of a Human Body *1913*
31¾″ × 25¾″ Galleria d'Arte Moderna, Milan

*It is still possible to discern suggestions of the human figure in this
work, but at first sight it reads as a bold and vigorous abstract painting.
The energetic interlocking forms create a spiral arrangement, but the
movement is less free and the colour more subdued than in the other
painting on the same theme (p.97).*

Scala

Portrait of Ferruccio Busoni *1916*
69¼″ × 47¼″ Galleria Nazionale d'Arte Moderna, Rome

*Boccioni stayed with the composer Busoni in the last months of his life
when he was on leave from the army. It was at this time that Boccioni
painted this portrait (he also did one of Busoni's wife), which shows a
new stylistic development, its massive forms and broken colouring
clearly recalling the work of Cézanne.*

The Futurist Dream

Created on a wave of outrageous publicity, Futurism was a popular artistic movement which glorified violence and technology and called for the destruction of libraries and museums.

Futurism was essentially the creation of one man – the poet Filippo Tommaso Marinetti, whose galvanizing spirit and frenetic energy earned him the nickname 'The Caffeine of Europe'. When, in 1909, Marinetti launched his *Founding and Manifesto of Futurism*, there was no Futurist Movement as such. The Manifesto was a massive publicity stunt, designed to attract the attention of artists in Italy and France, and to encourage them to declare their allegiance to Marinetti's ideas.

Marinetti's aim was to create a cultural revolution. The arts, he claimed, were living in the past, blinded by admiration for the forms and values of classical culture. These had no relevance for the man of the new technological age. The time had come for a new art which would express the

ideals of a world transformed by science, above all the ideals of violent action, anarchy and revolt. Marinetti wrote: 'we want to free this land from its smelly gangrene of professors, archaeologists, and antiquarians . . . we will sing of great crowds excited by work . . . of the polyphonic tides of revolution in the modern capitals, of the vibrant nightly fervour of arsenals and shipyards blazing with violent electric moons.'

Although Marinetti and the Futurists claimed to be revolutionary, few of their ideas were in fact wholly original. Many of their favourite themes – the idea of the artist as hero, the glorification of violence, the rejection of academic culture and the support of anarchy, had been discussed in French Symbolist literature of the late 19th century, in the

Private Collection

Leaders of Futurism
(below) The Manifesto of Futurist Painters *was published in 1910 and signed by some of those shown here: Russolo, Carrà, Marinetti, Boccioni and Severini. They promised a revolutionary art inspired by 'the world transformed by victorious science'.*

Girl Running on a Balcony (1912)
(right) Giacomo Balla was Boccioni's teacher and joined the Futurist movement in 1910. He was interested in the study of motion based on a photographic analysis of movement. In 1913, he put his works up for auction, announcing 'Balla is dead'.

Fabbri

Museum of Modern Art, Milan

Umberto Boccioni

Red Horseman (1913)
(left) Carrà's painting sums up all that appealed to the Futurists: the glorified warrior on his horse symbolizing heroism, dynamism, and aggression. Ironically, it was painted at a time when Carrà was drifting away from Futurism through disagreements with Marinetti and Boccioni and a growing interest in Cubism.

works of writers such as Mallarmé and Valéry.

The novelty of Futurism lay primarily in its mass appeal. From the start Marinetti aimed, not just at a handful of cultured elite, but at as wide an audience as possible. Using newspapers, leaflets and public demonstrations, the Futurists set out to command the attention of the public as a whole, approaching the spread of artistic ideas as if it were a political campaign.

One of the Futurists' most ambitious projects took place in Venice, where Marinetti and his friends climbed the bell-tower of St Mark's armed with a loudspeaker and a trumpet, and hurled abuse at the churchgoers leaving Mass. The notorious Futurist Evenings were designed to reach a mass audience and drew people from all strata of society. Marinetti described the audience at an evening held in February 1910 as a mixture of 'ultra-pacifist clerical conservatives' and 'workers bellowing like the threatening waters of a dam'.

The Futurists' outrageous behaviour was not, however, simply designed to draw attention to themselves. Their aim was to provoke an active response from the audience, to replace the passive spectator and the privileged critic with a public that was actively involved in judging art.

As well as revitalizing Italy's culture, Marinetti aimed to create a new language, a dynamic language, free from the restraints of traditional

Boccioni: Caricature of a Futurist evening

grammar, syntax and verse-forms. Already, in 1905, he had launched his own literary magazine, *Poesia*, which provided a forum for the avant-garde and which also published many of the Futurist manifestos. In 1912, he published the *Technical Manifesto of Futurist Literature*, which began: 'Sitting on the gas tank of an aeroplane . . . I sensed the ridiculous inanity of the old syntax inherited from Homer.' Marinetti introduced the idea of Words-in-Freedom, a free use of language allowing the poet's imagination free rein. Released

Futurist Evenings
(above) These were theatrical evenings calculated to rouse the audience – usually to anger. The performance consisted of manifesto reading, poetry and provocation – and success depended on the level of abuse, not applause.

101

brilliant colours and dynamic lines.'

In its early years, the Futurist movement was radically anti-feminist. Marinetti's first manifesto exalted 'scorn for women' and declared war on 'moralism, feminism, and every opportunistic and utilitarian cowardice'. Over the next few years, however, Marinetti, for one, successively adapted his position, moving to a more general attack on the traditional Romantic view, not only of women, but of marriage and the family, as threats to the individual, whether male or female.

Nonetheless, Futurism remained aggressively masculine in its ideals, and the images of women presented in Futurist literature and painting are conventional ones, either of the traditional

Futurist music

The main contributor to Futurist music was the painter Luigi Russolo, whose homage to Music *(right) shows swirling crescendos. He believed that beyond the conventions of music lay a vast range of untapped sound, from Nature to the roar of machines. He invented the Noise Intoners (above) to reproduce some noises of the modern world – and was greeted with whistles and boos.*

from traditional rules, he would manipulate words 'to render every vibration of his being'.

It was perhaps the Futurist painters who were faced with the most difficult task in finding a technical formula to express their ideas. The *Manifesto of Futurist Painters* preceded the production of any Futurist works of art, and gave little idea of what a Futurist painting would look like. Ultimately, the painters all interpreted the Manifesto in different ways, and did not develop a homogeneous Futurist style.

All the painters, however, shared a preoccupation with movement, and with depicting the 'dynamic sensation' of life. They also aimed to discard the conventional idea of the passive spectator, remote and detached from the work of art. 'The spectator must in future be placed in the centre of the picture', they triumphantly declared, but it was only Boccioni who consistently achieved this, using his device of 'lines of force'.

THE FUTURISTS AND SOCIETY

Futurist activity was not simply confined to the traditional fine arts. One of Marinetti's aims, in fact, was to extend the boundaries of conventional culture, and to break down the barriers between art and everyday life. The Futurists published manifestos on Noises, Smells, Sex and Fashion, as well as Painting, Sculpture and Music. In 1913, Giacomo Balla published the *Futurist Manifesto of Men's Clothing*, describing the desired image of the Futurist man. Futurists must fight, he wrote, 'against all forms of lifeless attire which makes man feel tired, depressed, miserable and sad . . . against so-called "good taste" and harmony, which weakens the soul and takes the spring out of the step. We must invent Futurist clothes, hap-hap-hap-hap-happy clothes, daring clothes with

Estorick Collection, London

mother-figure, or of the prostitute and the femme fatale. Furthermore, despite their vociferous protests, both Marinetti and Severini married, and Boccioni seems to have led a life of comfortable domesticity with his mother.

Few women were actively involved in Futurism, the most notable exception being the French writer Valentine de Saint-Point who, in 1913, published the *Futurist Manifesto of Lust*, which declared that 'Lust, when viewed without moral preconceptions and as an essential part of life's dynamism, is a force.'

By 1914, the interests of the Futurists had begun to diverge. For a while, however, they were to some extent reunited by the excitement preceding the outbreak of the war, and by their own activities in promoting Italy's entry into the conflict. From the start the Futurists had glorified war, which Marinetti described as 'The Sole Hygiene of the World'. They were also staunchly nationalistic – one of Marinetti's aims had been to assert the cultural supremacy of Italy over France, which had long held a position of cultural dominance in Europe. It was thus almost inevitable that the Futurists would have supported the Interventionist cause. In many respects, in fact, Futurism came uncomfortably close to Fascism – in its worship of technology, its exaltation of physical violence, and its glorification of youth.

The war effectively ended Futurism. When it was over, Marinetti attempted to reform and revitalise the Movement, but his most gifted followers were either dead, or had simply deserted the cause. The premature death of Boccioni deprived Futurism of one of its most talented spokesmen, and the Futurism which lingered on was a poor shadow of its former self.

Mattioli Collection, Milan

63⅝" × 61½"; oil on canvas, with sequins

Dynamic Hieroglyphic of the Bal Tabarin/Collection, The Museum of Modern Art, New York

Interventionist Manifesto (1914)

(above) Carrà's painting reflects the Futurists' support of Italy's intervention in the Great War. The Futurists' last action as a group was to go off to war, many of them joining the speedy cyclist Battalion.

Dancers at the Ball (1912)

(left) These dancers are one in a series in which Severini explored the disintegration of form to express movement. In this, he was influenced by Cubism.

Marchesa Casati

(right) The Futurists advocated 'scorn for women', but the Futurist Marchesa was the femme fatale type they had rejected in theory. Her soulful eyes inspired the work of both Marinetti and Balla.

Scala

A Year in the Life 1911

The Futurist celebration of war and dynamic action appeared to be echoed officially in 1911 when Italy seized her chance to launch an attack on Tripoli while Europe was already entangled in the second Moroccan crisis. Meanwhile, China was starting on the revolutionary road that was to lead to Communism.

In the spring of 1911, Boccioni and the other Futurist painters put on their first major group show at the Free Exhibition of Art in Milan. By November, when they were visiting Paris to see 'where things stood in art', the Italian government had acted with an ardour that might have been Futurist-inspired, attacking Tripoli (modern Libya) and proclaiming its annexation. As Tripoli was part of the Ottoman Empire, this entailed war with the Turks, who were only forced to yield in 1912, when they were confronted with a still more serious crisis in the Balkans.

The Italians timed their action carefully, taking advantage of a crisis that left the European powers disinclined to interfere. A series of anti-foreign disturbances in Morocco gave the French an excuse to enter Fez and tighten their grip on the country.

Coronation Durbar
(above) On 12 December 1911, six months after his Coronation, George V and his wife, Queen Mary, presided over a great Imperial Durbar at Delhi. Here it was announced that the Indian capital was to be transferred from Calcutta to Delhi.

Invasion of Tripoli
(right) Italy had long cast covetous eyes on Turkish Tripoli, but it was not until the Agadir Crisis of 1911 that she had the opportunity to put desire into action. Italy declared the annexation of Tripoli on 5 November after concerted local Arab resistance.

This went beyond the rights granted them in 1906, after the first Moroccan crisis, and prompted the German government to send the gunboat *Panther* in July to the Moroccan port of Agadir, ostensibly to protect German interests. The new crisis generated a wealth of bluster – from Lloyd George, who in his Mansion House speech declared that Britain would not be treated 'as of no account', and from the Kaiser, who asserted that the German navy would ensure 'a place in the sun' for his empire. In reality neither the French nor the Germans wanted war, and in November matters were adjusted on a *quid pro quo* basis. France was given a completely free hand in Morocco; the Germans, pacified by territory in the Congo, agreed to the establishment of a French protectorate in Morocco.

A revolt that had been long brewing against the ruling Manchu dynasty in China finally flared up on 10 October, after an explosion in Hankow gave away the location of the revolutionary headquarters and their arsenal. The subsequent abdication of the Manchu dynasty and foundation of a republic was only the beginning of China's troubles. Intermittent civil war was the order of the day until the Communist victory of October 1949.

LIBERAL TRIUMPH OVER THE LORDS

Meanwhile, Britain finally resolved the constitutional conflict which had begun in 1909, when the House of Lords rejected Lloyd George's Budget. This had made H. H. Asquith's Liberal Government determined to end the House of

Great composer
(right) The Moravian born composer, Gustav Mahler, died in Vienna of heart disease on 18 May 1911, a few weeks short of his 51st birthday. His intense experiences of joy, pain and sadness during a turbulent life were poured into his symphonies and lieder, written during summer holidays; the rest of his time being taken up with his work as a conductor.

Archiv für Kunst und Geschichte

Bildarchiv Preussischer Kulturbesitz

Jean-Loup Charmet

Nationalist revolutionary
(above) Dr Sun Yat-sen had long been working for the overthrow of the corrupt and outmoded Manchu ruling dynasty. However, when revolution broke out in 1911, the Doctor was in America raising funds for the cause. He landed at Shanghai on 25 December and was elected provisional President, only to hand over two months later to the ambitious General Yuan Shih-K'ai. China's astonishing revolution was only just beginning.

Gunboat diplomacy
(right) When rebel Moroccan tribesmen attacked Fez early in 1911, the Sultan called on French military help. Germany responded by sending in a gun-boat, the Panther, *to the Moroccan port of Agadir, claiming the French action was contrary to the Algeciras agreement of 1906. After months of diplomacy, an agreement was signed in November whereby Germany gained French territory in the Congo in return for guaranteeing the French protectorate in Morocco.*

Lords' absolute veto on legislation; but it could only do so through legislation which had to be passed by the Lords themselves. After two elections and protracted parliamentary infighting, Asquith was able to tell the Lords that, if necessary, the King would create a sufficient number of Liberal peers to ensure that the Bill passed. Since the Conservatives had a huge majority in the House, the peerage would be 'cheapened' by hundreds of new creations – an intolerable prospect that persuaded the Lords to pass the Parliament Bill, which left them only the power to delay legislation for two years.

The year 1911 was also Coronation Year for King George V, who had succeeded Edward VII in 1910. The new King then visited India, hoping to counteract the spirit of subversion by holding a Durbar – a splendid occasion on which the royal couple, surrounded by attendants carrying peacock fans, yaks' tails and golden maces received the homage of the Indian princes. Among the 'boons' announced by the King was the transfer of the Indian capital from Calcutta to Delhi.

Also during this year, a revolution led by Francisco Madero in Mexico overthrew the 35-year-old régime of Porfirio Diaz. The Norwegian Roald Amundsen reached the South Pole on 11 December, seven weeks ahead of Captain Scott's party, and Pyotr Stolypin, the Russian premier, was assassinated. The *Mona Lisa* was stolen from the Louvre and only recovered in 1913. Wassily Kandinsky and Franz Marc founded *Der Blaue Reiter* group of painters in Munich. H. G. Wells poked fun at the Fabians in *The New Machiavelli*, and D. H. Lawrence published his first novel, *The White Peacock*.

Stolen masterpiece
(left) On 11 August, Leonardo's celebrated painting, Mona Lisa, *was stolen from the Louvre, an event which is used to poke sly fun at the* amours *of the French Under-Secretary of State in this contemporary cartoon: the multitude of Mona Lisas in the drawing all bear faces of famous actresses of the day. The painting was recovered when the thief, an Italian called Vincenzio Perugio, offered it for sale to an antique dealer. Perugio had been able to walk out of the Louvre with the canvas under his coat.*

Jean-Loup Charmet

The Fagus factory
(right) Walter Gropius (1883-1969), the German designer and architect, started work on the Fagus shoelace works at Alfeld-an-der-Leine near Hanover only a year after setting up his own architectural practice. Completed in 1914, the building was ahead of its time and is still striking today. The glass curtain walls which continue around the corners of the building, the flat roof and overall functional elegance created a landmark in the history of architecture. The factory is now preserved as a national monument.

Bildarchiv Preussischer Kulturbesitz

Private Collection

AMEDEO MODIGLIANI
1884-1920

The life of Amedeo Modigliani was short, unsettled and tragic. From the intellectual stimulation of his family home in Livorno, he moved to Paris where he lived in extreme poverty, consoled by drink, drugs and a succession of lovers. Here he met other painters and poets but shied away from the avant-garde, developing his own highly individual style. He submitted to the influence of only one painter, Cezanne.

Although Modigliani was prodigiously talented as both painter and sculptor, he sold little during his lifetime. This poverty contributed to his weak health as did his bohemian lifestyle. Hoping he would benefit from the sun, his dealer sent him and his pregnant mistress to the South of France. But Modigliani died a year later. His gift was to unite traditional artistic values with the modern spirit.

The Bohemian Artist

Modigliani's romantic sensibilities and careless disregard for his health in his intensive pursuit of his artistic talents, led him to fulfil the tragic role of the handsome but doomed youth.

Amedeo Clemente Modigliani was born on 12 July 1884 in the Italian Mediterranean port of Livorno. Rumour had it that the Modigliani family were once bankers to the popes and that his mother was descended from the great philosopher, Spinoza. Modigliani encouraged these elaborations which, as usual, contained a degree of truth.

Amedeo's father, Flaminio, was a businessman who was ruined in the year the boy was born. Flaminio's commercial failure forced him to travel widely and Amedeo's mother, Eugenia, was left to run the household. Both were Sephardic Jews, that is people who were originally descended from the Jewish settlers in Spain. As part of their faith,

the Modigliani family respected their ancient traditions and valued a liberal education. In the eyes of the Livorno bourgeoisie, Eugenia was unconventional: she drank tea (an English practice), wrote literary articles and did translation work. This was more practical than progressive for she kept an extended family, and Dedo (as Amedeo was called) was the youngest.

The young Modigliani grew up in a lively and stimulating environment, soon developing a variety of cultural interests way beyond his years. His mother introduced him to the Romantic and Symbolist poets like Leopardi, Wilde, Baudelaire and Rimbaud. Through his aunt Laure, he became

A pampered child
(left) This photograph shows Eugenia Modigliani with her youngest child Amedeo, then only 13 months old. Eugenia doted on Dedo, as the family called him, and indulged him partly because of his poor state of health.

Bulloz© DACS 1987

Jacques Thomas/Explorer

Private Collection

acquainted with the philosophy of Nietzsche who wrote of the artist exiled from society by his creative genius and intuitive nature. Later, during his years in Paris, Modigliani would chant poetry to his friends – verses as elegant and self-contained as his paintings.

Modigliani was a spoiled and capricious child, partly because he was a beautiful-looking little boy, and partly because of his fragile health. In the summer of 1895, he developed pleurisy and, in 1898, he suffered a serious attack of typhoid. In the same year, his mother wrote in her diary: 'On the first of August, [Dedo] begins drawing lessons . . . He thinks he's already a painter; as for me, I don't really want to encourage him, in case he completely neglects his studies to pursue this shadow.' Modigliani joined the art class of Gugliemo Micheli in 1898, and soon afterwards formed a breakaway art group. But late in 1900, tuberculosis aggravated by an attack of pleurisy was to put an end to his studies.

FRESH SURROUNDINGS

During a period of convalescence, Modigliani travelled to Naples, Amalfi and Capri and later to Rome and Venice. With his health restored, he left his home town in 1902 to study first in Florence, and then in Venice, where he made many friends – among them the painter Umberto Boccioni – and studied the work of the old masters, Bellini, Titian and Carpaccio.

In January 1906, Modigliani left for Paris, determined to chance his luck as a portrait painter. Here he enthusiastically adopted a similar bohemian lifestyle to that he had sampled in the old quarters of Venice. He used stimulants, mostly

Utrillo: Le Lapin Agile/Musée National d'Art Moderne

Montmartre
(above) Modigliani arrived in Paris in 1906, and went to live in Montmartre, a haven for artists since the 1880s. The 'dusty and romantic' cabaret, Le Lapin Agile (depicted here by Utrillo) was where artists gathered to the strains of popular songs.

Italian origins
(left) Modigliani grew up in the Mediterranean port of Livorno, a lively commercial centre of little artistic interest.

Drinking companion
(right) The painter of Montmartre scenes, Maurice Utrillo, joined Modigliani on his notorious drinking bouts.

Archiv für Kunst und Geschichte/Painting © DACS 1987

Key Dates

1884 born in Livorno

1900-1 suffers a severe attack of pleurisy; tours Italy to recuperate

1902-6 studies briefly in Florence, then in Venice

1906 arrives in Paris

1909-14 concentrates mainly on sculpture

1914 meets Beatrice Hastings

1917 meets Jeanne Hébuterne; Zborowski, his dealer, arranges first solo exhibition

1918-19 travels to south of France; first child born

1920 dies in January; Jeanne commits suicide

artist. He affected an artistic style of dress, 'always in chestnut corduroy, with a brilliant scarf around his neck and with a broad felt hat', as a friend described him, and he despised Picasso's functional workman's overalls. Modigliani's painting, too, was old fashioned, an uncertain synthesis of the styles of Impressionism, Toulouse-Lautrec and Art Nouveau. These were years of experiment and self-discovery. A memorial exhibition of Cézanne's work was held in 1907 and soon Modigliani was imitating Cézanne's way of suggesting form and space through colour. This new preoccupation with form led to his first essays in sculpture. Between 1909 and the outbreak of war in 1914, he produced few paintings. Working next door to the sculptor, Constantin Brancusi, his attention focused on an ambitious and ultimately unrealized, sculptural

hashish and alcohol, maybe in an attempt to overcome his characteristic shyness. Even so, his first French patron, a young doctor called Paul Alexandre, remembered 'a very well brought up young man', who did most things in moderation.

After a few weeks of luxury in a comfortable hotel, Modigliani began to lead a nomadic existence, moving from one lodging house to another, first in Montmartre, then south of the Seine in Montparnasse. The small allowance his mother sent was insufficient to support a life spent increasingly in bars and brothels. Unable to pay his bills, he gave away pictures and did hack work, making portraits in cafés for a few francs.

Paris made Modigliani sensitive to his Jewish origins; and he discovered spiritual and artistic affinities with the 'peintres maudits', the 'accursed painters', who were mostly Jewish, stateless and poor. Unlike these artists, Modigliani had been trained, and had had a relatively liberal upbringing. His experience was very different – there had been neither ghettos nor anti-semitism in Livorno – but he shared these artists' insecurities in a foreign city that did not welcome destitute artists, least of all Jewish ones.

UNREASONABLE BEHAVIOUR

Distressed by his continual financial hardships, Modigliani's behaviour began to deteriorate. He was expelled from Dr Alexandre's artists' community for destroying other members' work: he would become aggressive in discussions on Cubism, the new movement which had ousted Fauvism, and had to be ejected by Libion, the *patron* of the café La Rotonde. Modigliani seemed to be conforming to his adolescent literary inspirations, and also to Nietzsche's ideas of alienated genius. He had anticipated as much in 1901, when he observed in a letter to a friend: 'People like us have different rights from other people because we have different needs which put us . . . above their morality'.

During these early years in Paris, Modigliani was living an outmoded, 'decadent' image of the

Jean-Loup Charmet

Patron and friend
(above left) The dealer
Zborowski (seen here on
the right) gave immense
support to Modigliani
and, at the artist's earnest
request, also took his
friend, the Jewish emigré
painter, Soutine, (seated
on the left) under his
wing.

Beatrice Hastings
(left) Modigliani's stormy
affair with the South-
African-born writer,
Beatrice Hastings, whom
he painted several times,
began in 1914. They
drank and took drugs
together, she matching
his excesses with her own
eccentricities.

La Ruche
(above) During the war
years, Modigliani worked
in a small studio in La
Ruche ('The Hive') – a
twelve-sided building
which became the refuge of
many bohemian artists,
among them the
unsophisticated Soutine
and the Russian, Chagall.

project of which the completed *Caryatids* (p.115)
formed only a small part.

Modigliani served his real apprenticeship
during these years. The demands he made on his
weakened constitution were evident to his mother
on his return to Livorno in 1909. She indulged him
and bought him a new set of clothes. That he had
changed was clear to his former art school friends
when he made another visit to Livorno in 1912.
One observer described him as follows: 'His head
was shaven like an escaped convict . . . He was
wearing a miserable linen jacket and open shirt
and his trousers were held up by a string'. He
showed his companions photographs of his
sculpture: they said he was mad, and jokingly
suggested that he dump them. Modigliani had
never felt so artistically isolated.

When Beatrice Hastings, the South African
journalist known to her Montparnasse neighbours
as the 'English poetess', met Modigliani in 1914, it
was not his art – she, also, considered it
unexceptional – that attracted her, but his
appearance. He was 'the pale ravishing villain' in
corduroy. Beatrice gave Modigliani his first
sustained relationship. It was a gladiatorial affair
with her able to match Modi (as the artists named
him) both in wilfulness and in her capacity for
drugs and drink.

Beatrice's affair with Modigliani coincided with
a vulnerable period in his life. His deep regret at

The Impoverished Artist

Modigliani appears to have lived in conditions of extreme poverty soon
after his arrival in Paris. He occupied a succession of cheap rooms in
Montmartre; then, having moved south of the Seine in 1909, he found
cheaper lodgings in Montparnasse. His allowance from home was too
small to buy art materials as well as the hashish and absinthe on which
he had become dependant. When he turned actively to sculpture, he
reputedly stole sleepers from the new Metro line nearby for wood to carve;
and many of the *Caryatids* were created from stone blocks removed from
construction sites by night, or lifted from the road surface.

Mary Evans Picture Library

The dedicated sculptor
(right) During his early
years in Paris, Modigliani
devoted most of his
energies to sculpture.
Unlike Rodin, Picasso
and Matisse, he was
never interested in
modelling in clay, which
he regarded simply as 'too
much mud'. He carved
wood and stone,
producing a series of busts
and figures which were
strongly influenced by
African and Oceanic
sculpture. In 1914, he
abandoned the medium,
partly because carving
exhausted him and was
bad for his fragile lungs,
and partly due to lack of
materials.

Night refuge
(left) This strangely
decorated café in
Montmartre provided a
refuge for poor artists,
offering food and shelter.

Tate Gallery, London

111

Bridgeman Art Library

Private Collection

Last love
Modigliani met Jeanne Hébuterne while she was an art student and she later bore him a daughter. The affair was as tempestuous as that between Modigliani and Beatrice Hastings, but Jeanne was a less volatile adversary. Sadly, the liaison was to be a tragic one – heavily pregnant with their second child, Jeanne leaped to her death from a fifth-floor window shortly after Modigliani's death.

their apartment, in a state of shock, having been bitten in the testicles. By 1915, Modigliani had become increasingly dependent on drugs, while Beatrice, unable to curb his excesses, was now a virtual alcoholic. A year later, their relationship was completely exhausted.

In July 1917, Modigliani met Jeanne Hébuterne, a talented 19-year-old student at the Académie Colarossi. He painted her portrait more than any other, and she bore him a daughter, Jeanne. Her relationship with the artist was as stormy as Beatrice's had been: stories of her ill-treatment in public places by Modigliani are numerous. Unlike the poetess, however, Jeanne was timid, devoted and suffered his infidelities.

Success remained elusive in Modigliani's last years, although a market was cautiously growing, encouraged by Leopold Zborowski who had succeeded Guillaume as Modi's dealer in 1916 and who hawked canvases round Paris by foot on occasions to interest collectors. Indeed, it was not easy to see Modigliani's work for he took part in few exhibitions.

A SENSATIONAL SHOW

In December 1917, his first one-man show was staged at the Berthe Weill gallery. Modigliani had, by that time, received scant notice from the press: even the seven sculpted heads included in the Salon d'Automne of 1912, passed largely unnoticed. Zborowski was therefore keen to

his gradual drifting away from sculpture was compounded by the privations of the First World War. He was often ill; his allowance from home ceased; he was exploited by unscrupulous speculators. Many of his friends were at the Front and the cafés were left to foreigners and invalids.

Yet, paradoxically, his portraits achieved their familiar harmony and greatest insight during the War years. Modigliani was encouraged by the dealer Paul Guillaume, who bought all his works and rented a studio for him. Here, he painted his famous series of nudes, though he seems to have rarely portrayed his lovers in this way.

Modigliani's affair with Beatrice continued to be particularly stormy and violent. Their arguments often deteriorated into physical fights. On one occasion he actually threw Beatrice out of the window and, on another night, he rushed out of

Café Society

'Tell me where you eat and I'll tell you how you paint' went a popular song in the early years of this century, for cafés were the social centres of Paris. Places like La Rotonde and the Dôme provided an important forum where avant-garde painters and sculptors could meet and share ideas. Modigliani was familiar in many Parisian bars where he would make rapid sketches, sell them and buy something to eat and drink.

H. Roger Viollet

admiration for Cézanne, and also painted his first landscape, as far as we know, since his student days in Italy. He was accompanied to Cagnes-sur-Mer by his friend, the painter Soutine, who produced several wild landscapes starkly at odds with his companion's tautly composed images.

Towards the end of his life, Modigliani became more superstitious when working, refusing to allow his studio to be cleaned or disturbed as if this might threaten his fragile talent. This uncertainty was probably provoked by his lack of success: financial well-being meant little to him, but self-respect was essential.

Modigliani contracted pneumonia in the bitterly cold January of 1920. After drinking all night in the local bars, always ending up at La Rotonde, he would roll out into the icy air of the early hours in just his shirt sleeves. Contemporaries described him on these occasions as 'very drunk, abusive and terribly emaciated'. A few days before his death, he collapsed in the studio he shared with Jeanne, and the terrified young girl sat watching him dying, without thinking of sending for a doctor. On January 24 he died of tubercular meningitis. He was 35.

Jeanne's tragedy is inextricably linked with Modigliani's. Several months pregnant with his second child, she threw herself from an upstairs window at her home soon after his death. Five years later, her body was moved from the bleak cemetery near Bagneaux, and she was buried beside Modigliani at Père Lachaise.

Cagnes-sur-mer
Encouraged by his dealer Zborowski, who even paid for the trip, Modigliani went to Cagnes-sur-Mer in the south of France in April 1918. He was accompanied by Jeanne and other artists, including Soutine.

attract visitors and put several nudes in the window, which unfortunately faced a police station. Equipped with special powers in wartime, the police objected to the 'obscene' display and closed the exhibition on its opening day.

Zborowski was a Polish poet sympathetic to the 'peintres maudits'. He could afford to give Modi a small allowance although he sold little; and to organize a trip for his artists to the South of France in April 1918. Here Modigliani rediscovered his

Informal showcases
(right) Cafés provided cheap food and shelter from unheated and unserviced studios, also giving artists the opportunity to meet. When artists had money they were big spenders, otherwise patrons would accept a painting in settlement of bills, thus turning their cafés into informal showplaces. Cafés were also where artists held their wild fancy dress balls.

At the Dôme
(left) The Dôme was a café in Montparnasse much frequented by Modigliani, here seen in relaxed pose with his elbow on the table during a discussion with the part-time picture dealer, Adolphe Basler.

Rusinol: Cafe de Montmartre/Museu d'Art Modern de Montserrat, Barcelona

Tradition with Modernism

**Despite his limited subject matter of portraits and nudes,
Modigliani's work was unique in its combination of traditional
form with new painting techniques.**

Portraits and nudes established themselves as Modigliani's subjects from the beginning, (he painted only a handful of landscapes). He was not concerned with portraying realistic appearances, but expressing the feeling and mood of his models, especially in relation to himself. Most often, in the early part of his career, tension and anxiety were the recurring motifs, probably echoing those features in his own life at the time.

Living as a poverty-stricken foreigner in Paris brought its own insecurities compounded by his feeling of alienation from the avant-garde artists. His lack of money meant shortage of materials, so his paint was spread thinly and he had to use both

The young artist
(below) Modigliani was enrolled at art school in Livorno at the age of 14. This charcoal sketch, prominently signed by him, could be a self-portrait. But in any case it is a wonderfully sensitive drawing showing the artist's remarkable talent.

Seated Nude (1916)
(right) This is one of the artist's earliest nudes. Her torso is drawn naturalistically – only her face is painted in Modigliani's mannered style. Warm red or brown tones usually surround his nudes, but here the predominant colour is a cool blue.

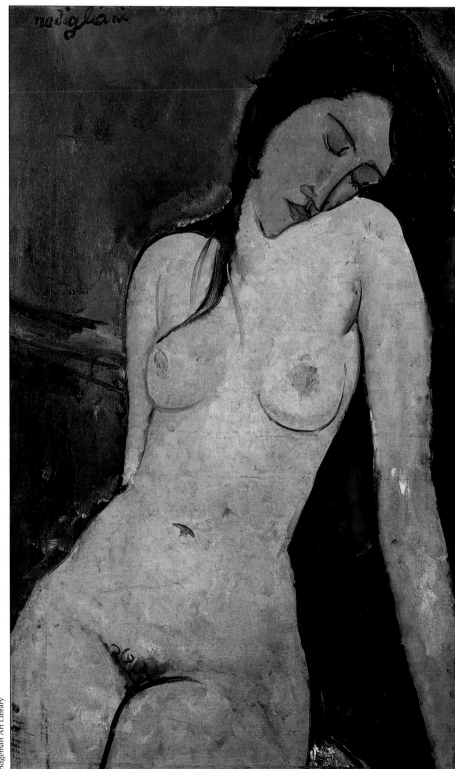

Private Collection   Courtauld Institute Galleries, London

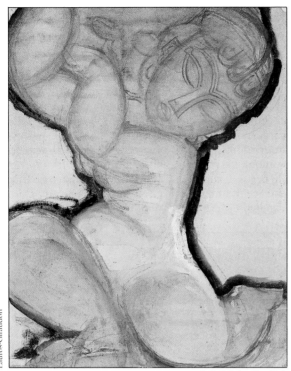

Perls Galleries, New York

Caryatid (c.1913)
(left) Modigliani planned a sculpture of a crouching caryatid and did a series of watercolour sketches in preparation. They were ideas rather than actual designs, for, like this one, they could not be translated into stone without collapsing.

Landscape at Cagnes
(below) Modigliani's rare landscapes were done in the South of France. Working with Soutine, Modigliani may have been affected by the other's passion for landscape.

their monumentality: one never forgets the rough-hewn limestone block from which they have emerged. They also show a preoccupation with the primitive sculptures of Africa and Oceania which Modigliani shared with his contemporaries.

Modigliani had always considered himself a painter-sculptor, having made his first sculpture at Carrara in 1902, symbolically close to the quarries that had provided Michelangelo with stone. In Paris, he carved the blocks that had been begged or stolen from building sites. But he had never received any training in sculpture and possessed neither the discipline nor the strength (the dust irritated his lungs) to complete his ambitious project to construct a temple to humanity adorned with pillars in the form of Caryatids. Unable to find materials in wartime, he ceased sculpting in 1914. The experience inevitably fed his art, giving him a sure sense of form. In fact, his painting began to take on the characteristics of his sculpture,

sides of the canvas. Nonetheless, certain characteristics emerge as trademarks of his style as early as 1908, fixing his own personal identity as an artist, and these are refined into the elegance and poise of his last pictures. In his portraits sloping shoulders and slender necks support gently tilting heads in which small mouths, long noses and dark, introspective eyes are caught in a hypnotic expression.

From Italy, Modigliani carried with him the influences of Symbolism and *Stile Liberty* (Art Nouveau) and his early works reflect this in mood and in their linear pattern. But in Paris, Modigliani discovered Cézanne at his retrospective exhibition in 1907, and his debt to Cézanne is revealed in the construction of his compositions – in the arrangement of forms and isolation of planes through colour – as well as his choppy brushstrokes. Although Cézanne had opened a new direction in art leading to Cubism, he had never lost respect for the integrity of the human form, which became central for Modigliani.

SCULPTURE OUT OF STONE

On his return from summer in Livorno in 1909, Modigliani had decided to realize his deep-seated ambition to become a sculptor. This is how he had introduced himself on his arrival in Paris three years earlier. Between 1909 and 1914 he produced barely twenty pictures. Inspired by the Rumanian sculptor, Brancusi, whom he met in 1909 and next to whom he had a studio for a couple of years, Modigliani was at work during these years on the remarkable heads that integrate the concern for mass, volume and form that had initially attracted him to Cézanne. The force of these mysterious faces lies in their inscrutable expressions, and in

Landscape at Cagnes (1919) Private Collection

115

especially the modelled faces of his last portraits. The regret at this failure must have cut deep. For in the combination of aggression and finesse that carving demands, Modigliani may have found the best vehicle for his art of personal feeling.

In his portraits Modigliani showed keen insight into the character of the sitter, a reflection of his own personal opinion. But his approach to nudes was different – he rarely painted lovers naked. Instead he used unprofessional models, preferably servant girls. Interestingly, he always painted nudes in series, showing he was working on them exclusively over a period of time.

His nudes are blatantly sensual and self-confident and stand in the tradition of the genre, alongside those of Titian, Goya and Renoir. Warm colours enhance the sensuous undulating line that encloses the female form, buffeted by animated brushstrokes. Unlike his portraits, their facial expressions seem all to be the same.

His confident use of line marks out the countless drawings Modigliani made through his career. They were *aide-mémoires* in which interesting compositions were stored to be reused sometimes years later, although he never dispensed with a model. Drawing was primarily the preliminary to painting. Jacques Lipchitz recalled Modigliani making lots of drawings

COMPARISONS

Stylized Images

When attempting a realistic image, an artist uses colour in a natural way and tries to portray exactly what he sees. In a stylized image, however, colour is used for emotional effect. Distortion is often used to emphasize a particular point; in Parmigianino's *Madonna*, the long, curved neck combined with the downward glance and overstated gesture present an image of grace and tenderness. Modigliani distorted features to show up certain characteristics of the sitter.

Manoukian Collection, Paris

Fernand Khnopff (1858-1921)
Who Shall Deliver Me?
(above) According to Symbolist tradition, women are mysterious and predatory. Here, the Belgian painter Khnopff expresses this through the woman's Sphinx-like enigmatic smile and her hypnotic gaze. The paleness of her face and her fixed stare are reminiscent of death which, in Symbolist imagery, is linked with woman and love.

Uffizi, Florence

Parmigianino (1503-40)
Madonna with the Long Neck
(left) In this religious painting, the artist sought to portray refinement through the elongation of his figures, softened by a serpentine curve.

rapidly, seldom stopping 'to correct or ponder'. He would familiarize himself with his sitter in this way, and gradually decide on a pose. When he subsequently turned to the canvas, he worked quickly, 'interrupting only now and then to drink from a bottle standing nearby'. His friend Lunia Czechowska noted that he worked best in a rage, stoked by cheap brandy or rough red wine. The act of painting required an immense emotional investment from the painter, who would move about, sigh deeply and cry out in frustration. He worked intensively in order to complete the picture at only one sitting.

A year before he died, Modigliani went to the

The Elongation of Head and Neck

Modigliani relied on a linear graphic style influenced by his early enthusiasm for Art Nouveau and used elongation to enhance the expressive quality of his line. His long faces, too, reflect the African masks newly discovered by the art world. But Modigliani used the device of elongation to convey many different qualities of character, from arrogance to grace, depending on how he saw his sitter.

National Gallery of Art, Washington, Chester Dale Collection

Gypsy Woman with Baby (1919)
(above and detail left) This portrait was painted when Modigliani was in the South of France. Warm and cool colours are strongly juxtaposed, particularly in the blue blanket wrapped round the baby, held fast by its mother's suntanned hands (detail). Behind the mother and child, the sun shimmers on the wall.

South of France. As models he used local people and it may be that his impending paternity moved him to use children as subjects. Here, too, he painted his rare landscapes. All of them feature houses and trees – he seemed to shy away from untouched nature. Despite his dislike of the Mediterranean outdoors, his paintings during this period have the airy luminosity of the South.

Modigliani's contribution to modern art lies in his individuality. Unlike the artists of the avant-garde, for example Picasso, he was not concerned with fragmenting form but in the integrity of form in keeping with the tradition of the past. Yet his modernity is reflected in his use of compositional devices which make his portraits appear new and unique – after all, it is impossible to confuse his work with any other artists. Having no school, Modigliani has no successors.

THE MAKING OF A MASTERPIECE

Portrait of Jacques Lipchitz and his Wife

Both Lipchitz and Modigliani were Jewish, middle class and sculptors, but they do not appear to have been close friends — which the portrait seems to reflect in the formality of its composition.

In 1916, Lipchitz commissioned a portrait of himself and his new wife, Berthe, from Modigliani, who informed him, 'My price is ten francs a sitting and a little alcohol'. To familiarize himself with his sitters, Modigliani made numerous drawings and the next day, set to work on an old, primed, canvas. Working intensely, he had finished by the end of the afternoon. Lipchitz wanted to pay him more, and so asked him to paint more 'substance'. 'If you want me to spoil it,' came the reply, 'I can continue'. Modigliani gave another fortnight to the picture.

Lipchitz did not like his portrait and kept it in a closet until, in 1920, soon after Modigliani's death, he exchanged it for some of his own earlier sculptures.

Helen Birch Bartlett Memorial Collection/Art Institute of Chicago

Stadt Kunstmuseum, Duisberg

> 'Your real duty is to save your dream.'
>
> Modigliani

The Guitar Player (1918)
(left) Jacques Lipchitz (1891-1973), born in Lithuania, trained as an engineer before settling in Paris in 1909 and becoming a sculptor. At the time that Modigliani painted his portrait, he was experimenting with Cubist principles in three-dimensional form, using interlocking planes to cause light to reinforce the sense of solidity.

Jacques Lipchitz
(right) Lipchitz was an ambitious and highly skilled sculptor on his way to success when he commissioned this portrait, which may explain why Modigliani sees him as bourgeois. When Modigliani died, it was Lipchitz who made his death mask.

Marlborough Fine Arts Ltd, London

Preliminary drawings

(left and right) Modigliani made several sketches of Lipchitz and his wife in different poses, separately and together. In the end he based the composition of the portrait on a wedding photograph. The drawings are quick and perfunctory, but show how easily Modigliani can capture a mood and pose in his fluent line.

Private Collection

Berthe Lipchitz

(right) The sculptor's new wife is beautiful with her large dark eyes and full mouth. However, Modigliani was not in sympathy with her and her expression comes over as decidedly smug. Her blank gaze gives her no connection with the outside world.

Gallery

Modigliani's range of subjects as a painter was small. With the exception of a few landscapes, he virtually confined himself to portraits and female nudes, but in both these fields he ranks among the greatest artists of the 20th century. His reclining nudes in particular – a serene but sensuous example of which is shown here – include some of

The Equestrienne (L'Amazone) *1909*
36¼″ × 25½″ Private Collection

This portrait was a commission obtained through Modigliani's friend, Paul Alexandre. The sitter – a baroness – was a renowned horsewoman. Modigliani admired the most successful society portraitists of his day, his countryman Boldini and the American Sargent, but as this picture shows his own talent was far too original to express itself through conventional glamour and flattery. He brilliantly captures the baroness's haughtiness and her pride in her riding habit, which he changed to yellow at the last moment, displeasing the sitter. She must have wanted a more conventional image as she rejected the picture.

the most majestic images in modern painting.

In his portraits, Modigliani ranged more widely than in his nudes, painting men, women and children with equal mastery and varying his approach greatly. His portraits of children, for example The Little Peasant and Little Girl in Blue, show how delicate he could be, but often he incisively exposes the shortcomings of his sitters' characters, depicting Jacques Lipchitz and his Wife as a rather smug and self-satisfied couple. And in the Portrait of Jeanne Hébuterne, painted shortly before his and her death, he showed that he could attain to great heights of spiritual intensity.

Scala

Portrait of Frank Burty Haviland *1914*
28¾″ × 23½″ Gianni Mattioli Collection, Milan

Haviland was a wealthy collector of Anglo-French parentage, who also tried his hand at painting. Modigliani painted this portrait soon after he returned to painting from sculpture and in it seems to express a delight to be once again working with colour. The broken colours perhaps owe something to the example of Seurat, but they are used much more exuberantly.

The Bride and Groom *(1915-16)*
21¾″ × 18¼″; oil on canvas. Collection, The Museum of Modern Art, New York

*Modigliani's pictures almost invariably portray single figures – this
double portrait and the one opposite are rare exceptions. The sitters
here are not identified, but Modigliani presents them as vulgar and
pompous, poking fun at bourgeois pretentiousness. The stylized
treatment of the faces reflects the influence of Cubism.*

Portrait of Jacques Lipchitz and his Wife *1916-17*
31½″ × 21″ Art Institute of Chicago

The couple are placed close to the frame and by having Jacques rest his hand possessively on Berthe's shoulder, the two are brought together. Their pose is formal, like the wedding photograph from which it derives. However, the graceful contours of faces and clothes soften their stiffness, and strike a contrast with the verticals behind them.

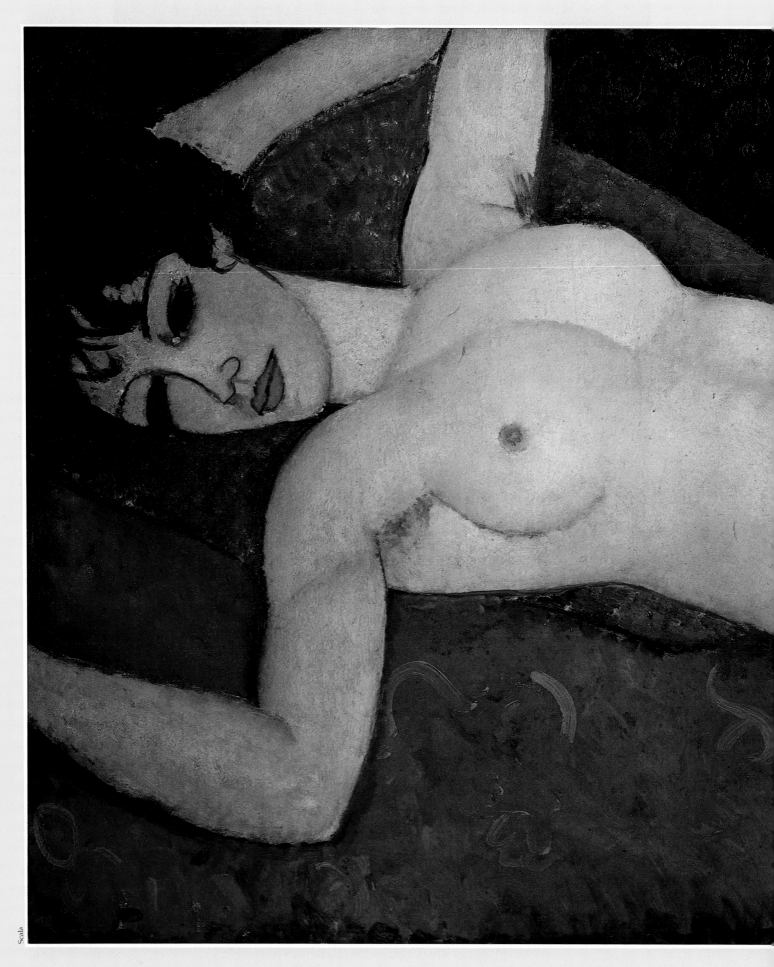

124

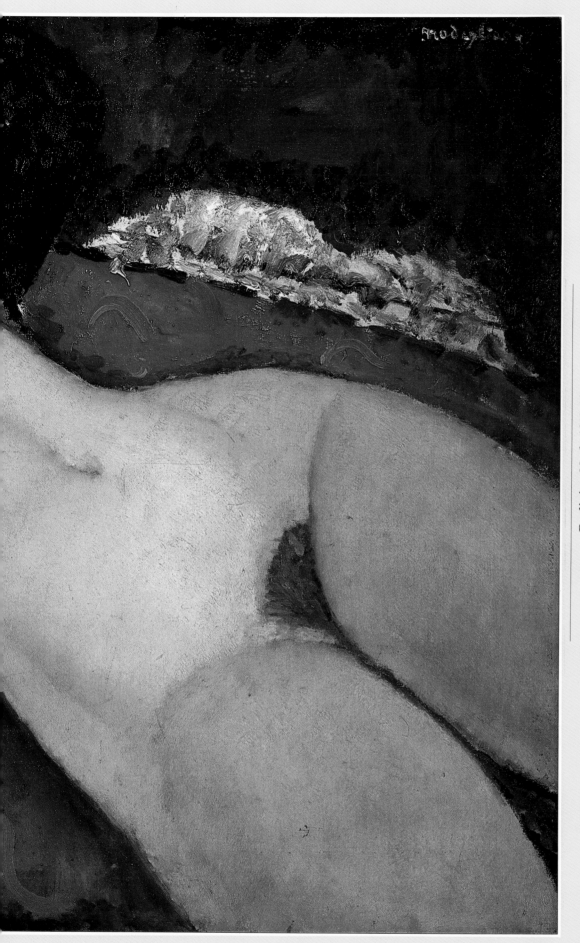

Reclining Nude 1917-18
23½" × 36¼" Gianni Mattioli Collection, Milan

The reclining nude is a theme that has inspired some of the greatest artists from the Renaissance onwards, and Modigliani is undoubtedly the tradition's greatest upholder in the 20th century. His treatment is usually openly erotic and often – as here – the woman is seen in close-up. In this, one of his finest depictions of the subject, Modigliani shows not only his mastery of expressive contour, but also his skill as a colourist, the model's skin resonantly set off against the reds and blues of the background.

126

A Seated Man Leaning on a Table 1918
24″ × 39″ Private Collection

An unusual feature of this painting is the presence of the table, bottle and glasses – Modigliani rarely used props such as this, preferring to concentrate his attention purely on the sitter. Other aspects of the picture, however, are typical of Modigliani, notably the blank eyes, which here give the sitter a rather distracted, far-away look, as if he has paused from his drinking to muse over some problem. As well as simplifying the eyes, Modigliani has schematized the nose in a way fairly common with him, showing it almost in profile even though the head is seen virtually full-face.

The Little Peasant *1918*
39½″ × 28½″ Tate Gallery, London

The title is Modigliani's own. This picture was painted in the South of France and it brings to mind some of the portraits that Cézanne (an artist for whom Modigliani had the greatest admiration) painted in Provence. Its utter directness and the use of colour, rather than line or shadow, to suggest modelling, recall the great French master.

The Little Girl in Blue *1918*
46¼″ × 28½″ Private Collection

*Modigliani painted children with great tenderness, but without
sentimentality. The solemn little girl is painted more naturalistically
than in many of Modigliani's pictures of this date – the eyes, for
example, are depicted with some detail, rather than as the slits he
often used. The lighting, too, is unusually soft for Modigliani.*

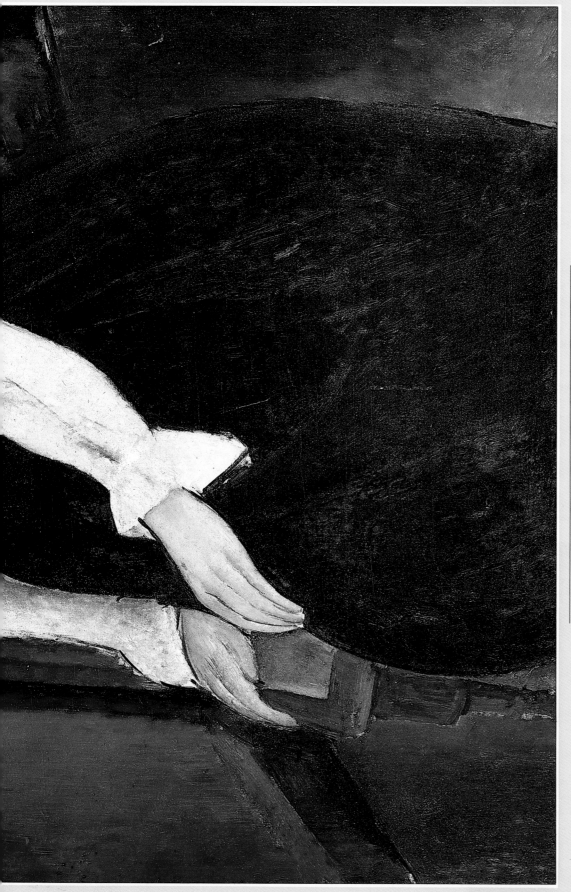

Portrait of Jeanne Hébuterne 1919
51¼″ × 32″ Private Collection

This is one of Modigliani's last and most moving paintings. His mistress is shown pregnant with their second child, as she was when she committed suicide the day after Modigliani's death in January 1920. Even without reading into it our knowledge of their imminent tragic end, the painting has an extraordinary sense of tension and unease, this coming as much from the twisting, almost dizzying pose as from her blank and pallid expression. It is a fitting memorial to a career that more than that of almost any other 20th-century artist embodies the idea of doomed genius.

131

The Ballets Russes

While Modigliani was working in Paris, the city was thrilled by the arrival of the Ballets Russes – the Russian troupe that created a spectacular ensemble of music, dance and design.

'I never saw anything so beautiful', wrote Marcel Proust, quite simply, after first seeing the Ballets Russes in 1910. Proust's reaction was shared by thousands of his contemporaries. Under the direction of Sergei Diaghilev, Parisian audiences were amazed to see ballet no longer as a vehicle for virtuoso dancing solos, but as a theatrical ensemble within which dancers, designers and composers were given equal weight. 'Ballet can only be created by the very closest fusion of these three elements', declared Diaghilev, and it was his genius as a manager to make the Ballets Russes a forum for every hope of artistic experimentation.

Diaghilev's success is more remarkable for the fact that he had not, in his early life, demonstrated any great interest in dance. Living in St Petersburg, his real loves were music and painting. But although he was committed to

The great Diaghilev *(below left) Called 'the collector of geniuses' it was Sergei Diaghilev who, almost single-handedly, masterminded the Ballets Russes. Gathering around him the finest dancers, artists and composers in the world, he had an unerring gift for realizing the creative possibilities in every form of art. After Diaghilev's arrival in Paris, the world of traditional art and dance was transformed and was never to be the same again.*

developing these arts in Russia, it was to Paris that he looked for inspiration. In 1906, he realized his dream of conquering the city by presenting a major exhibition of new Russian painting at the Salon d'Automne. It was a great success, and the visit encouraged him to introduce concerts of Russian music to the Parisians the following year, and a Russian opera – Mussorgsky's *Boris Gudonov* – in 1908. The rapturous reception that Diaghilev's productions met was already beginning to dictate the future course of his career.

A REVOLUTION IN BALLET

Meanwhile, in St Petersburg, Diaghilev had grown aware of the enormous creative possibilities of ballet. He had met Léon Bakst, the costume designer and Alexander Benois, the set designer, and shared in the excitement generated by Isadora Duncan in her visit to Russia in 1905. This American star was a dancer who rejected the conventional movements of classical ballet, bringing to dance the freedom of expression that was to be found in the acting of Stanislavsky and the music of Stravinsky. Shortly afterwards, the brilliant choreographer, Mikhail Fokine, began to develop ways within which expressive dancing

John Longstaff; Diaghilev

AIDE DE CAMP   ZOBÉIDE

LE GRAND EUNUQUE

'An angel, a genius'
(left) 'His lightness of limb is controlled by a tremendous muscular power, so that when he leaps into the air he appears to float.' So wrote one critic of the inimitable qualities that were to make Nijinsky the most famous male dancer in the history of ballet.

A lavish spectacle
(right and below) The Oriental extravagance of the set and costumes of Schéhérazade, marked the pinnacle of Leon Bakst's career as a designer. Never before had the West seen such lurid juxtapositions of colour, or so exotic a recreation of Persian myth. With music by Rimsky-Korsakov, Nijinsky took the part of the Golden Slave in a sequence based on the Thousand and One Nights. *Inspiring a craze for Eastern designs, Schéhérazade became the most popular of the Ballets Russes' repertoire.*

Giraudon

could be made the basis of an entire ballet. The result was *Le Pavillon d'Armide*, first performed in St Petersburg in 1907. Recently returned from Paris, Diaghilev was enthralled and longed to take the production to Paris. He set down to work with Fokine, Benois and Bakst, and, in 1908, the nucleus of the Ballets Russes was formed.

Masterminded by Diaghilev, their plan was to present an ambitious and varied repertoire, including not merely *Le Pavillon d'Armide*, but Fokine's *Les Sylphides* – composed around the orchestrated works of Chopin – and the powerful Polovstian dances of Borodin's *Prince Igor*. Using predominantly Russian composers – Glinka, Stravinsky, Borodin, Rimsky-Korsakov, Mussorgsky, Tchaikovsky, Glazunov – it was Diaghilev's vision to bring together talents from every field of art and create a balanced world of illusion and entertainment, a theatrical echo of the exoticism launched by Gauguin some twenty years earlier. Undeterred by the fact that he was unable to use Paris's main theatre, the Opéra, Diaghilev had the ramshackle Théâtre du Châtelet especially redecorated throughout, while he prepared, 'inwardly faint with fear and doubt', for the opening night of his creation, the Ballets Russes, in May 1909.

It was a night that was to change the course of European ballet. The Russians' brilliance, as witnessed by an illustrious audience from all over Europe and America, had Paris on its knees begging for more. Fokine's dynamic choreography had elevated the art out of the sterile style of the Imperial Ballet and the Paris Opéra forever. In Karsavina, Diaghilev had a ballerina of genius, an equal, in many ways to Pavlova, who joined the Ballets Russes for the latter part of their spectacular first season. But most sensational of all was the rediscovery of male dancing which in the Ballets Russes, was thrust centre stage.

The greatest of all these dancers was Vaslav Nijinsky, who had been a child prodigy in St Petersburg. Nurtured by Diaghilev, who was his lover, he was able to develop his unique combination of technical virtuosity and magnetic stage presence. By the time he reached Paris with

SCHÉHÉRAZADE

ALMEE

AIDE DE CAMP DU SCHAH

SHARIAR ROI DES INDES ET DE CHINE

ALMEE

ALMEE

NEGRE

133

the Ballets Russes, no other dancer of his generation could match him in his quality of movement, or his gift of completely merging himself in all his roles. Such roles, under Fokine's direction, would always emphasize his androgynous vitality and included the poet of *Les Sylphides*, the stuffed puppet in *Petrushka*, and the half-animal slave in *Schéhérazade*. To the astonished Paris audiences, Nijinsky became instantly, 'an angel, a genius'.

SPECTACULAR DESIGN

This was the first time, too, that the West had seen design as one of the composite arts of ballet staging. And for the first season, it was the brightly coloured work of Léon Bakst which brought a dramatic suggestiveness of its own to the performances of the Ballets Russes. For *Schéhérazade*, for example, Bakst turned to Persian art to create the exotic background of a harem, painted in lavish expanses of emerald, red and blue. On its opening night, the audience burst into applause at their first glimpse of it.

Bakst, of course, was not the only designer

A vital partnership
(above) Igor Stravinsky wrote the music for many of the Ballets Russes' finest ballets, including The Firebird, Petrushka *and* Le Sacré du Printemps.

Prima Ballerina
(left) Described as 'the most exquisite daughter of classical choreography', the beautiful Tamara Karsavina was the first ballerina of the Ballets Russes to haunt Western audiences. Her modesty and intelligence made her a favourite with Diaghilev, to whom she remained loyal throughout. Here she is seen in the title role of The Firebird, *first performed in 1910. She would dance the entire ballet à pointe – floating ethereally across the stage on the tips of her toes.*

Jacques Emile Blanche: Tamara Karsavina/Musee d'Opera, Paris

whose talents Diaghilev was to utilize. His unerring gift for recognizing genius, led him to attract the services of almost every major artist of his day, including Picasso, Matisse, André Derain, Joan Míro, Georgio de Chirico, and many others. Diaghilev's concern was that the ideas behind the Ballets Russes should be constantly renovated and developed, so that 'dance should express the whole epoch to which the subject of ballet belongs'. It was this principle which led Diaghilev to stage *Parade* – a Cubist burlesque, based on a book by Jean Cocteau, with designs by Picasso, choreography by Massine and music, including

NIJINSKY
dans "La Péri"

Aquarelle de Léon BAKST.

Bakst: Nijinsky dans 'La Péri'/Bibliotheque Opera, Paris

Magical design
(left) It was for the Ballets Russes' first season in Monte Carlo in 1911, that Bakst designed this superb programme. It shows Nijinsky in La Peri, *a ballet dropped when the company returned to Paris.*

Diaghilev's legacy
(below) The gifted Russian dancer, Serge Lifar, seen here with Lubov Tchernicheva and Felia Dubrovska, was Diaghilev's last protegé. He later became a key figure in the Ballets Russes de Monte Carlo – a company set up to continue the spirit of Diaghilev's original troupe.

Pavlova, Diaghilev was left short of audience-drawing stars and deeply in debt.

In spite of these difficulties, Diaghilev was to retain the impetus of the Ballets Russes as the springboard of modern dance. The choreographer, George Balanchine, the male star, Serge Lifar, the young British prodigy, Alicia Markova, and the designer, Georges Roualt, were amongst those who worked on the outstanding ballets of Diaghilev's last years – *Le Chatte, Apollo* and *The Prodigal Son.*

With Diaghilev's sudden and untimely death in 1929, the original Ballets Russes company disbanded. But his legacy had already begun to be disseminated throughout the world. Markova returned to England, Lifar to France, and Balanchine travelled to America – each creating of the Ballets Russes tradition an independent success. In 1932, René Blum initiated a Ballets Russes in Monte Carlo, with the banner, repertory, and some of the senior artists (including Fokine) of the original company. Today, the importance of the Ballets Russes to everyone working in dance theatre cannot be over estimated – they owe what they are doing to Sergei Diaghilev.

the sounds of a typewriter and a hooter, by Eric Satie. First performed in 1917, the traditional audiences were scandalized. But to an extent, they relied on Diaghilev to shock them.

The troupe, however, was barely to survive the First World War. Nijinsky, who had replaced Fokine as principal choreographer, had been dismissed in 1913 when he announced to the jealous Diaghilev that he was going to be married. Tragically, he was to dance for the last time in 1917 – after a mental collapse, he spent the rest of his life in an asylum for the insane. Without Nijinsky, Fokine, and the legendary ballerina, Anna

H. Roger Viollet

Modigliani went to Paris in 1906, the year that France's longest-running scandal, the Dreyfus affair, finally came to an end. During this year France was also to emerge safely from the Moroccan crisis, while in strife-torn Russia, the Tsarist regime struggled hard to regain control.

For over a decade the Dreyfus case had torn France apart, pitting republicans and socialists against royalists, clergy and the military; it had ruined many friendships and even divided families. 'The Affair' began in 1894, when a Jewish army officer, Captain Alfred Dreyfus, was convicted for betraying military secrets to Germany and sent to Devil's Island off French Guiana. As Dreyfus was a wealthy man who had no motive for such a betrayal, there was a suspicion that justice had miscarried and within two years new evidence pointed to a different culprit, a Major Esterhazy. The Army General Staff refused to admit its error for political reasons, and colluded with Esterhazy who was tried and triumphantly acquitted by a military tribunal. The Deputy Chief of the Secret Service, Colonel Henry, had perpetrated a series of forgeries and cover-

Lords Gallery, London

Jean-Loup Charmet

Bibliothèque Nationale

Conservative attack on Free Trade
(left) For some years Britain had become increasingly aware that her status as the 'workshop of the world' was losing ground to foreign competition; America and Germany had become the new industrial giants of the 20th century. In 1903, Joseph Chamberlain, the former Conservative Colonial Secretary, began to campaign against Free Trade, the basic tenet of Victorian commercial faith, arguing instead for trade protectionism, excepting imperial goods. Tariff reform rapidly became the issue of the day, splitting the Conservative Party and being chiefly responsible for the Liberal landslide victory in the 1906 General Election. Free Trade was now safe under a Liberal government, but defeat made the issue of tariff reform official Opposition policy until 1913. In 1914, Lloyd George was able to announce an exceptionally prosperous year which vindicated the maintenance of the status quo. Protectionism would have upset Britain's rising new source of income from invisible exports such as banking.

ups to preserve 'the honour' of the Army, but even when Henry was unmasked and committed suicide, a new court martial in 1899 again found Dreyfus guilty. Although his innocence was by now so obvious that he was pardoned by the French President, it took another seven years before a court of appeal declared, on 12 July 1906, that Dreyfus had been wrongfully convicted.

GERMAN DEBACLE

Two European crises which had begun the previous year were resolved in 1906. The Morocco crisis had arisen when Germany had opposed French and Spanish ambitions in the Sultanate, thus forcing the resignation of the French foreign

minister, Delcassé. However, in a fluid international situation the Germans could not make up their minds whether they wanted to bully or conciliate France, and the final outcome of the negotiations was an international conference at Algeciras in the early months of 1906. Here, only Austria-Hungary supported Germany, and France was able to go ahead and take over the police force and State Bank of Morocco. Germany was humiliated, and the Anglo-French military conversations provoked by the crisis served to strengthen the *entente cordiale*.

In 1905, the Tsar had seemed helpless in the face of a revolutionary crisis sparked off by Russia's terrible defeat in the war against Japan. The high point of the 1905 Revolution occurred in October of that year, when a general strike and peasant unrest had forced the Tsar to grant a constitution. Riots

Dreyfus rehabilitated
(left) Captain Alfred Dreyfus (right foreground), the innocent victim of political intrigue and anti-semitism in a spy scandal that rocked France for more than a decade, was finally rehabilitated in 1906. In a quiet ceremony on 21 January at the Ecole Militaire, he was solemnly reinstated and awarded the Croix de Chevalier de la Legion d'Honneur *on the same parade ground from which he had been ignominiously drummed out of the army 12 years before. Dreyfus fought for France in the Great War and died in 1935.*

Giancarlo Costa

Jean-Loup Charmet

Count Witte and the Duma
(left and above) Sergie Witte's talents as an administrator and statesman led him to be appointed Russia's first Prime Minister in November 1905. A month before, he had urged Nicholas II to accept the October Manifesto to pacify nationwide anarchy and revolt. The Tsar was thus forced to concur with the establishment of a national government, the State Duma, which on paper would turn the Tsarist régime into a constitutional monarchy. Witte, *determined on no such thing, was dismissed five days before the first session on 10 May 1906 due to his unpopularity with the court. The Duma immediately pressed for wide-ranging reforms which the Tsar found 'totally inadmissible'. They followed up with a vote of no confidence in the government who in turn dissolved the Duma on 21 July. Nevertheless, three further Dumas were to sit before the dramatic outbreak of the Russian revolution in 1917.*

and mutinies continued throughout 1906, but the government gradually reasserted control, and thousands of revolutionaries began the long, hard journey to Siberia. The first Russian parliament, the Duma, met in May and, although elected on a limited franchise, began to voice demands for true representative government, equality before the law and the right to strike. Ten weeks later the Tsar's troops surrounded the Duma and it was dissolved. The more radical deputies retired to Viborg in Finland and called on the people to refuse taxes and military service, but their appeal had little effect. In June, the ruthless and reactionary Pyotr Stolypin became premier and initiated a thoroughgoing policy of repression, order was restored, and for a few years it seemed that the Tsarist autocracy had triumphed over the forces of revolution.

In Britain, the Liberals, with support from the Labour Representation Committee, later to become the independent Labour Party, won a landslide victory at the 1906 General Election. Committed to a programme of reform, they began with the Trades Disputes Bill, which legalized peaceful picketing and gave protection to trade union funds from employer's claims for compensation after strikes.

In 1906, the great painter Paul Cézanne died. One playwright, Samuel Beckett, was born; another, Henrik Ibsen, died. The longest of all railway tunnels, the 20-kilometre Simplon Tunnel linking Italy and Switzerland, was opened and the latest word in naval progress, HMS *Dreadnought*, was launched. This big-gunned giant gave its name to an entire class of battleships and set off a new round in the arms race.

Giancarlo Costa

Algeciras Conference
(left) In 1905, Kaiser Wilhelm had attacked the validity of a French mandate in Morocco, calling for a conference through which he hoped to break up the Anglo-French entente. *He presumed that his official demand for equal international trading rights in Morocco would attract American support, while Spain and Italy would fall into line. In August, the Kaiser attempted to detach France from the* entente cordiale *by offering Moroccan concessions and the opportunity to join his new but shortlived treaty alliance with Russia. Britain meanwhile pledged military support to France. The three-month conference began in January 1906. The outcome was a disastrous blow to German prestige.*

Military manoeuvres
(below) Kaiser Wilhelm's erratic foreign policy was inspired by fear and ambition. Germany had become fearful of 'encirclement' and consequently increasingly saw a preventive war as necessary for survival. A growing sense of nationalism and a desire for a foreign empire to vie with the great European powers led her to build up her naval and military might. Here the Kaiser confers with his newly appointed Chief of Staff von Moltke and King August von Sachsen during a military exercise in 1906.

Archiv für Kunst und Geschichte

GALLERY GUIDE

Matisse
Many of Matisse's paintings are now in the Hermitage, Leningrad, including *Dance* (p.21), along with the mask-like portraits of his wife (1913) and *The Moroccan* (1912). In the United States, much of his work is still in private hands. The Barnes Foundation (Merion, Pennsylvania) is particularly well-endowed, while there are examples in Chicago (*Woman & Goldfish,* pp.28-9) and Buffalo (*Music,* Albright-Knox Gallery). In his native France, there are major works in the Musée National d'Art Moderne, Paris, among them *Luxe, Calme et Volupté* (p.18). There is also a Matisse Museum at Cimiez (near Nice), where the painter lived and worked for much of his life.

Picasso
Picasso's output was so prodigious that there is scarcely a major modern collection which does not have an example of his work. In addition, there are three special museums devoted to him in France: in Paris, the Musée Picasso which contains his personal art collection, and in the south, the Château Grimaldi at Antibes and the nearby museum at Vallauris. In Madrid, the Casón del Buen Retiro has been converted into a permanent exhibition place for Picasso's masterpiece, *Guernica* (pp.64-5). *Les Demoiselles d'Avignon* (pp.56-7) is at the Museum of Modern Art, New York, which also owns his superb portrait of Gertrude Stein, and there is also a fine collection at the National Gallery of Art, Chester Dale Collection, in Washington. The artist is also well-represented in Cleveland, Chicago and Fort Worth.

Modigliani
The majority of Modigliani's paintings are either nudes or portraits. The latter are still in private hands. However, there are portraits of his first mistress, Beatrice Hastings, in Milan and in the Art Institute of Chicago, which also owns his remarkable double portrait of Jacques Lipchitz and his wife (pp.118-19). Modigliani's nudes are more widely dispersed, with major examples in Antwerp, Milan (pp.124-5) and New York (Museum of Modern Art). Late in his career, he produced paintings of children, of which *The Little Peasant* (p.128, Tate Gallery, London) is a notable example.

Boccioni
The greater part of Boccioni's works are split between Milan and Rome. The former has a particularly strong collection of his later work. At the Galleria d'Arte Moderna, there are experimental portraits, like that of Signora Busoni (pp.80-81), as well as still-lifes and good examples of his *Dynamism* series (1913). The same city also houses the best collection of his sculpture, including his vigorous striding figure (p.79) and his *Development of a Bottle in Space* (p.83) (both in the Mattioli Collection). Rome possesses his late portrait of Busoni (p.99) and several of his near-abstract depictions of horses. Outside Italy, there is a superb collection at the Museum of Modern Art in New York, including *The Laugh* (pp.84-5) and *The City Rises* (pp.92-3), and there are good examples in Hanover and London, where Estorick Collection contains the startling *Modern Idol* (p.96).

BIBLIOGRAPHY

G. Apollinaire (ed. L. C. Breunig), *Les Peintres Cubistes,* Collection Savoir Hermann, Paris, 1980

G. Ballo, *Boccioni,* Il Saggiatore, Milan, 1964

A. Bozollo and C. Tisdale, *Futurism,* Thames & Hudson, London, 1985

M. Calvesi and E. Coen, *Boccioni,* Electa, Milan, 1983

D. Cooper, *The Cubist Epoch,* Phaidon, Oxford, 1970

F. Elgar and R. Maillard, *Picasso,* Thames & Hudson, London, 1972

M. Giry, *Fauvism: Origins and Development,* Alpine Fine Arts, New York, 1981

L. Gowing, *Matisse,* Thames & Hudson, Oxford, 1979

D. Hall, *Modigliani,* Merrimack Pub. Circ., Topsfield, 1984

M. McCully, *A Picasso Anthology: Documents, Criticism, Reminiscences,* Arts Council and Thames & Hudson, London, 1981

C. Mann, *Modigliani,* Thames & Hudson, London, 1980

R. Penrose, *Picasso,* Penguin, London, 1971

W. Rubin, *P. Picasso: A Retrospective,* Museum of Modern Art, New York, 1980

W. Schmalenbach, *Picasso to Lichtenstein,* Merrimack Pub. Circ., Topsfield, 1985

P. Sichel, *A Biography of Amedeo Modigliani,* W. H. Allen, London, 1967

N. Watkins, *Matisse,* Phaidon, Oxford, 1984

Scala/Museum of Modern Art, Milan

The influential camera

(above) The invention of photography was of great importance to the development of modern art (see p.8). Giacomo Balla was particularly interested in photography, and Girl Running on a Balcony (1912) is the result of his study of motion based on a photographic analysis of movement.

Giacomo Balla (1871-1958)

The elder statesman of Italian Futurism, who taught both Boccioni and Severini. Born and educated in Turin, Balla was slow to establish his artistic career and made his living through portraiture and painting lessons. In fact, it was his pupils who prompted him to sign the Futurist Manifesto in 1910, although he did not exhibit with the group until 1913. Balla's art was strongly influenced by his interest in photography, as can be seen to comical effect in his Leash in Motion (1912, Albright-Knox Art Gallery, Buffalo) and in Girl Running on a Balcony (shown above).

Constantin Brancusi (1876-1957)

Romanian sculptor, active mainly in Paris. After training in Bucharest, Brancusi came to France in 1904 and worked briefly with Rodin. By 1907, however, he was more influenced by the primitive, curvilinear carvings of Gauguin and Derain, and he urged his friend, Modigliani, to work in a similar vein. Brancusi's mature style showed a preference for pure, organic forms, polished almost to the point of abstraction – so much so that in 1926 the US Customs charged duty on his Bird in Space, refusing to accept it as a work of art. His radical, simplified manner has had a huge impact on modern sculpture and proved a formative influence on the British Sculptor Henry Moore.

Georges Braque (1882-1963)

French painter, who pioneered the growth of Cubism. Braque was born near Paris, but was raised at Le Havre, in Normandy. He served an apprenticeship to a house decorator and then, in 1902, returned to Paris and enrolled in the Académie Humbert. Braque's first significant works were in the Fauvist style, but this was soon superseded by the influence of Cézanne. By 1909, he was closest to Picasso and, 'like mountaineers roped together', their partnership gave birth to the Cubist movement. Braque introduced several features, including the stencilled figures and the papier-collé variant of collage, which he created in 1912, but the outbreak of war ended their collaboration. Subsequently, he developed a more personal and painterly style. The most important works of his later career were the Studio series, which he began in 1949.

Robert (1885-1941) and Sonia Delaunay (1885-1979)

The creators of Orphic Cubism. Robert came from an aristocratic family and began his career by painting theatrical back-drops. His earliest works showed the influence of Pointillism and Fauvism, but his first major paintings, the Eiffel Tower series (1910-12), were thoroughly Cubist in style. In 1910, he married Sonia Terk, a Russia-born painter and textile-designer. Together, they developed a highly lyrical brand of Cubism, known as 'orphism', which emphasized the importance of colour and played down the role of nature. Epitomized by the series of Windows (1912), this influenced both the Italian Futurists and German Expressionists like Marc and Macke. After spending most of the War in Portugal, the couple became involved with the Dadaists, although their income was dependent on Sonia's design firm, the Atelier Simultané; this produced designs for clothes and books in bright colours and abstract forms. Their last joint commission was at the Exposition Universalle of 1937, for which they produced huge murals of up to 9,000 square feet.

André Derain (1880-1954)

Co-founder of the Fauvist movement. Derain was born near Paris and studied at the Académie Carrière, where he met Matisse. His early influences were Van Gogh and the Neo-Impressionists and, from them, he developed his taste for broad dashes of heightened colour. In 1905, he exhibited with Matisse and Vlaminck at the Salon d'Automne, where the term 'Fauvism' was coined. In the following year, he met Picasso and was one of the first to alert him to the possibilities of primitive art. After the Great War, Derain turned his attention to the example of Renaissance painting and, gradually, his work grew more conservative. During the 1920s, he received many commissions for ballet and theatre designs, but his reputation suffered considerable damage after his official visit to Nazi Germany in 1941.

Marcel Duchamp (1887-1968)

Avant-garde painter and theorist. Duchamp was born in Normandy, France, the son of a notary and the younger brother of another artist, Raymond Duchamp-Villon, an avant-garde sculptor also involved with the Section d'Or group. Marcel's earliest influences were Cézanne and the Cubists and, from 1912, his studio was the meeting place for the Section d'Or. At the same time, he was painting several versions of the Nude descending a Staircase, a key work which blended his Cubist technique with a Futurist emphasis on movement. The results proved too startling for the Salon des Indépendants (1912), but created a huge stir at the Armory Show, where the definitive version was exhibited in 1913. Duchamp soon abandoned his Cubist experiments to concentrate on structures like The Large Glass (the bride stripped bare by her Bachelors, even) (1915-23, Philadelphia Museum of Art); this technically complex work, which prefigured the Dada and Surrealist movements, made him famous. Divided into two horizontal zones and painted on glass, it expresses Duchamp's vision of the frustration of physical love. After creating this work, he devoted much of the later part of his life to chess.

Raoul Dufy (1877-1953)

French painter, a leading member of the Fauves. Dufy trained at Le Havre but spent most of his career in Paris. In 1908, he was at L'Estaque with Braque, producing landscapes that were closely modelled on those of Cézanne. However, Matisse was the greater influence and, through him, in about 1910, Dufy evolved his highly coloured decorative style. His exquisitely light touch was perfectly suited to the fashionable racecourse and esplanade scenes that were his favourite subjects and which he painted in both oil and water-colour.

Juan Gris (1887-1927)

Spanish painter working in Paris, who had a decisive effect on the development of Cubism. Born José González (Gris was a pseudonym), he trained initially as an engineer in Madrid, but left there in 1906 to pursue an artistic career in Paris. Gris settled in Montmartre, near Picasso, and began working as an illustrator, employing a decorative Art Nouveau style. His first paintings date from 1910 and, two years later, he was exhibiting with the Section d'Or group and making collages, after the fashion of Picasso and Braque. Gris was no imitator, however, and his experiments with overlapping forms – as in Homage to Picasso – helped to shape the growth of Synthetic Cubism. In the 1920s, he was commissioned to design sets and costumes for Diaghelev's ballets, but the hectic schedules played havoc with his health and he died at the age of forty.

Fernand Léger (1881-1955)

French painter who developed a very individual form of Cubism. Léger was raised in Normandy and trained as an architectural draughtsman. In 1907, he went to live at La Ruche, in Paris, where he came into contact with the Cubists. However, he preferred to exhibit with the Section d'Or group, where his debt to Cézanne became clear. After the War, Léger returned to figurative painting, evolving his distinctive, cylindrical forms (The Three Women in the Museum of Modern Art, New York, is a famous example). Later in his career, he designed theatre sets and murals for the Swedish ballet and, with Le Ballet Mécanique (1924), he created the first truly abstract film.

Gino Severini (1883-1966)

A leading member of the Italian Futurists. Severini was born in Cortona and worked initially as a book-keeper. In 1905, he organized the Italian Salon des Refusés with Boccioni and, the following year, he travelled to Paris, where he met Picasso and Braque. Severini's early style was influenced by Seurat and the Neo-Impressionists and he signed the Futurist Manifesto in 1910. However, he found the latter rather provincial and his own work showed a greater affinity with the Cubists. After the War, he followed the general trend for a return to classical values and this was underlined by his essay, From Cubism to Classicism, which was published in 1921. In later life, Severini was associated with the Novecento Italiano group, although he was very careful to distance himself from the Fascists.

Chaim Soutine (1893-1943)

Russian Expressionist painter, working mostly in Paris. Soutine was born near Minsk, the son of a clothes mender. His childhood was marred by extreme poverty, and his strict Jewish background – which forbade the making of images – hampered his early artistic ambitions. However, after training at Vilna, Soutine left for Paris in 1913, where he lived in penury at the colony of La Ruche. There, he met Chagall, Zadkine, Lipchitz and Modigliani, who painted his portrait (Staatsgalerie, Stuttgart). He also studied at the Ecole des Beaux-Arts. The filthy conditions Soutine worked in – he would keep painting a rotten slab of meat until the health inspectors confiscated it – and his quarrelsome nature earned him a reputation for eccentricity, which shows through in his intensely emotional canvases. His fortunes improved after 1923, when the American collector, Albert Barnes, purchased a large number of his pictures. His paintings have greatly influenced Francis Bacon.

Maurice Vlaminck (1876-1958)

Parisian-born painter, one of the original members of the Fauve group. Vlaminck came from a musical background – he played the violin – but began his working life as a professional racing cyclist (1893-6). He turned to painting in 1900, after an accidental meeting with Derain – whom he was to share a studio – although he was still obliged to support himself by playing as a musician in various nightclubs. His artistic independence was only achieved in 1906, when Vollard bought up the contents of his studio. Following his appearance with the Fauve group at the Salon d'Automne and on account of his work, he was described as a 'wild beast'. Vlaminck's main influence was Van Gogh, from whom he derived his thick slabs of pure colour; his The Bridge at Chatou is a typical product of his Fauvist period. His style did not progress far beyond Fauvism; he found Cubism sterile and considered Picasso to be a charlatan. Instead, his taste for stormy, threatening landscapes brought him closer to the Expressionists. Like Derain, his later career was marred by a trip to Nazi Germany in 1941.

INDEX

WITHDRAWAL